THREE ESSENTIAL BUSINESS TASKS

A short course in business basics for the busy entrepreneur working in an ever changing business environment

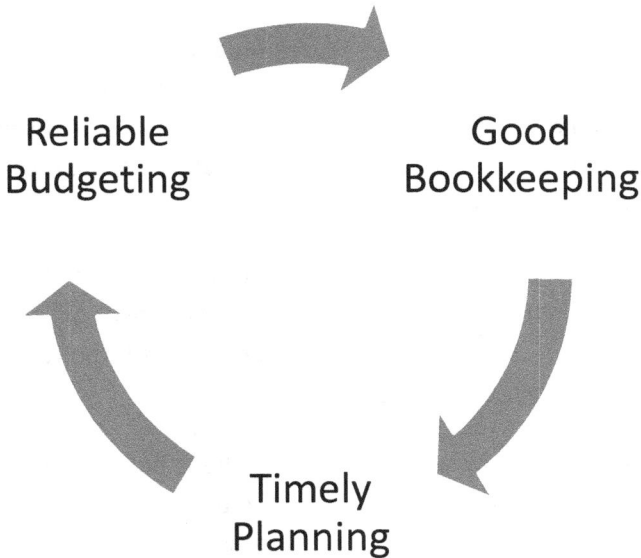

Reliable Budgeting

Good Bookkeeping

Timely Planning

A self-published book
By Robert Johnson

Retired just sharing what I have learned along the way

www.businessbasics-rj.blogspot.com
rwjohnson71@gmail.com

Writing is a unique talent. I have not mastered it but am attempting to. I have discovered that when you try to write a book; attempt to share what you have discovered over the years; ideas, events, and processes pop up, the source of which you have no clue.

So or Therefore (whichever is grammatically correct), I here and now thank all those writers, speakers, professors, employers, employees, and clients who have mentored me along the way. If I have used information gleamed from their insight and did not mention their name I apologize. Fifty plus years of learning is a long time.

What you will find in this book are a few recommendations that I believe will help you gain reasonable assurance of success in your business venture. But you will have to determine if the recommendations are applicable to your situation.

There are no guarantees presented here but experience has shown that an honest effort to improve what you do and how you do it has the potential of providing a pathway to success.

The Author

I have recently retired after some fifty plus years working my way through a business career. I started out shining shoes at an Air Force Base at eleven years old and ended my full time working career with my own Small Business Consulting venture. I currently work part time with a Not-for-Profit.

After twenty five years of working in 'Corporate America' I opened my own business that started as a bookkeeping service but it quickly became a consulting business focusing on the small business and not-for-profit community. I left the corporate world thinking I could make my life easier but quickly found out that 'ease' is a misleading term and definitely a misleading thought when you go into business for yourself. 'For yourself' is also misleading because you are never working *for yourself* when you start and own a business.

In a very short time I began to realize that small businesses and not-for-profit organizations needed help in a number of areas besides bookkeeping; areas that I had gained considerable experience in my corporate work. So I changed my business mission from bookkeeping to consulting.

In fifteen plus years I have seen the good, the bad, and the ugly in financial record keeping and general business management. But, I have also had the opportunity of watching businesses and not-for-profits grow once the owners and managers got a handle on the basics of being in business and doing business.

Retired now, I am sharing what I have learned (and am still learning) and have written my first book *Three Essential Business Tasks.*

Three guiding principles (some would call them a philosophy) I used in writing *Three Essential Business Tasks* are as follows:

There are no guarantees to success in business. But experience shows us that if you will do certain things correctly at the appropriate time, you will gain reasonable assurance of succeeding.   Author Unknown

In preparing for battle I have always found that plans are useless, but planning is indispensable.   General Dwight D Eisenhower

It is not the strongest of the species that survive, or the most intelligent, but the one most responsive to change.   Charles Darwin

Table of Content

THE AUTHOR..I

INTRODUCTION...V

TASK#1 GOOD BOOKKEEPING 1

Four Characteristics of Good Bookkeeping 1

How to maintain Good Bookkeeping even when the bookkeeper needs time off? 1

    1 Define what you want your bookkeeper to take charge of 2

    2 Create a Functional Chart of Accounts..................................... 4

    3 Create a COA Lexicon - A Transaction Posting Map 9

    4 Select the appropriate Bookkeeping Software 11

    5 Define the Software Functions you will use... 12

    6 Write Internal Financial Controls 13

    7 Write Bookkeeping Procedures 16

    8 Support your Bookkeeper 19

    9 Provide Skill Development Opportunities.. 21

    10 Create a Bookkeeper's Notebook 21

How to avoid financial abuse **22**

    The Problem with the Separation of Duties Principle 22

    Financial Review Process.. 23

Good Bookkeeping Summary...**24**

TASK #2 TIMELY PLANNING **25**

1 Identifying Change **26**

    Your Business Environment 26

    Your Business Cycle... 27

2 Choosing an approach to planning **28**

    Inactive Planning & Reactive Planning 28

    Pre-active Planning 29

    Proactive Planning... 29

3 Avoiding a common error in planning 29

4 Moving from the Start-up to an Operating Plan 31
    The Start-up Business Plan..31
    The Business Operating Plan...32

Timely Planning Summary.. 39

TASK #3 RELIABLE BUDGETING...41

1 Determine why you are going to create a budget 42

2 How to ensure reliable numbers 42

3 Use an Operating Budget Formula.. 44
    An Operating Budget Formula 44
    The Starting Point 45
    Building the Operating Budget...46

Using the Formula 52
    Service Based Business 52
    Product Based Business 54
    Business with Multiple Streams of Revenue..60
    Not-for-Profit Business 68

Budgeting Summary.. 72

CONCLUSION..73

Introduction

To gain and maintain reasonable assurance of success in a business venture there are certain tasks that require constant attention. Three of the tasks are the subject of this book.

- **Task #1Good Bookkeeping** – tops the list of three. With-out timely and reliable financial record keeping you will never know where you are in relation to your planning and budgeting. We don't discuss how to do bookkeeping but how to gain and maintain timely and reliable financial record keeping even when the bookkeeper needs time off.

- **Task #2 Timely Planning** – is next. "In planning for battle I have always found that plans are useless, but planning is indispensable". A quote from General Dwight David Eisenhower that captures the essence of this task. Planning and Re-planning includes evaluating where you are in relation to where you want to be; then writing or refining goals and related tactics to address the challenges you have uncovered.

- **Task #3 Reliable Budgeting** – is the third task. Before you can complete a timely and reliable budget you need Task #1 & Task #2 in place. In setting up your financial record keeping you establish line items for financially significant numbers you will use to evaluate business activity – budget line items. During planning you profile the numbers to get a handle on what it cost to be in business and what it cost to do business. These two sets of numbers make up your Business Operating Budget. An Operating Budget is your Business Plans presented in financial terms.

Getting to these three tasks requires two things: Setting aside time and a defined process. I have written *this book* to help you with the process; setting aside time is something you will have to work on.

Bookkeeping – The process of tracking money coming into a business and money going out of the business; verifying and recording transactions; securing source documents used to generate a transaction. <u>Purpose:</u> to enable a business owner (managers also) to evaluate business activity and make informed decisions.

Good Bookkeeping – All the above plus the following four characteristics:

1. **Efficient** – the right things are completed at the appropriate time;
2. **Effective** – the right things are completed correctly each time;
3. **Functional** – information recorded in the financial database is usable in defined formats;
4. **Uniform** – similar transactions are recorded using the same bookkeeping software function.

Planning – The process of identifying and defining change in the business environment that is having, that may have, that will in the near and distant future have an effect on being in business and doing business. Then, writing goals and related tactics to address the challenges of change.

Timely Planning – All of the above plus setting aside time each week and each month to review and refine plans to enable the business to stay ahead change.

Budgeting – The process of affixing numbers (dollars) to the goals and tactics written during a planning session.

Reliable Budgeting – All the above plus recognizing that budgeting will always be an educated guess at what you hope will take place in the near and distance future with an emphasis on educated guess.

Doing Business – Activity related to generating revenue.

Being in Business – Activity related to keeping the business open.

Task#1 Good Bookkeeping

Task #1Good Bookkeeping – tops the list of Three Essential Business Tasks. With-out timely and reliable financial record keeping you will never know where you are in relation to your planning and budgeting. We don't discuss how to do bookkeeping but how to gain and maintain timely and reliable financial record keeping even when the bookkeeper needs time off.

Four Characteristics of Good Bookkeeping

Over the years I have identified four characteristics that can be used to evaluate the quality of bookkeeping in a business.

1   **Efficient** – *the right things are completed at the appropriate time;*
2   **Effective** – *the right things are completed correctly the first time;*
3   **Functional** – *transactions recorded in the financial database are usable in defined formats;*
4   **Uniform** – *transactions are recorded using defined formats.*

How to maintain Good Bookkeeping even when the bookkeeper needs time off?

Here are my recommendations:

1. Define what you want your bookkeeper to take charge of;
2. Create a Functional Chart of Accounts;
3. Create a Chart of Account Lexicon
4. Select the appropriate Bookkeeping Software;
5. Create a Software 'Function' Lexicon
6. Write Internal Financial Control;
7. Write Bookkeeping Procedures;
8. Support your Bookkeeper;
9. Provide Skill Development Opportunities;
10. Create a Bookkeeper's Notebook.

Good Bookkeeping doesn't just happen; Good Bookkeeping has to be planned

1 Define what you want your bookkeeper to take charge of

A well written job description will focus on Responsibilities and Outcomes. Too often the bookkeeper's job description focuses on tasks. Tasks are important but they are (or at least should be) defined *in Internal Financial Controls* and *Bookkeeping Procedures*; documents the bookkeeper receives after they are hired.

Responsibility

What do you want the bookkeeper to take charge of?

> *The bookkeeper for xyz Company is the 'gate keeper' for company financial assets. Their primary responsibility is to ensure that:*
>
> - *Financial transactions have the appropriate source documentation and approval;*
>
> - *Financial transactions are recorded in a timely manner using defined procedures so that reports are uniform and reliable for making business decisions;*
>
> - *Source Documents used for financial transactions are secure and available for review by approved employees.*
>
> *As 'gate keeper' the bookkeeper has the written authority to deny or accept request to record a transaction. This authority is addressed in the Company's Internal Financial Controls. All employees including the business owner are expected to abide by the written controls. Any variance will need written approval by the business owner.*

Here is an important caveat to the above. You cannot relinquish financial responsibility to the bookkeeper. You can give the bookkeeper the task of maintaining the financial database, but responsibility for the

Good Bookkeeping doesn't just happen; Good Bookkeeping has to be planned

financial assets always stays with the business owner. See *How to avoid financial abuse.*

Outcomes

What do you want to see at the end of the day, the week, the month … from your bookkeeper's work?

Bookkeepers are not clairvoyant; they need to be told what you want to see at the end of the day, week, month… from their work? Most bookkeepers know even if they are not clairvoyant but the smart bookkeeper always asks the question, "What do you need from me to help you stay on top of your business; when do you need the information; and in what format?"

The smart business owner has prepared the list before hiring the bookkeeper and included it in the Bookkeeper's Job Description. The list should include who gets what, when, and how.

- Who defines the recipient;
- What defines the information;
- When sets the time;
- How defines the format.

Two critical questions for gaining and maintaining Good Bookkeeping even when the bookkeeper needs time off.

1. **What do you want your bookkeeper to take charge of?**
2. **What do you need from your bookkeeper?**

Good Bookkeeping doesn't just happen; Good Bookkeeping has to be planned

2 Create a Functional Chart of Accounts

A Functional Chart of Accounts will:

- Include line items (General Ledger Accounts) that summarize information of **financial significance** to analyzing business activity and making qualified business decisions;
- Provide the outline for financial reports;
- Provide a posting map for recording financial transactions.

Details are important but

Details are important in financial reporting but if you have too much detail you run the risk of chasing rabbits, nit-picking, creating confusion; if you have too little detail you won't have enough information to ask the right questions or make timely informed decisions.

This is where *'financial significance'* comes in – numbers that have meaning; that will help the reader of reports ask the right questions and lead to making informed decisions.

What information do you need to see on your Balance Sheet Report and on your Profit & Loss Report to enable you to analyze business activity, ask the appropriate questions, and make informed decisions?

The Balance Sheet Report Line Items

The 'Full disclosure principle' applies here. Full Disclosure simply put means that the Balance Sheet Report must contain information that will allow a reasonable person to make an informed decision about the 'condition' of a business at a specific point in time.

For the Balance Sheet this means that the line items on the report are fairly fixed; you don't have much leeway in deciding what to include. Bankers, Investors, Accounting Conventions, and of course the government are in control.

Three Essential Business Tasks

Good Bookkeeping doesn't just happen; Good Bookkeeping has to be planned

Work with an accountant to get the Balance Sheet list correct. The general format for listing Balance Sheet Line Items (General Ledger Accounts) is:

- **1000 Assets** – What the business owns
    - **Current Assets** – Assets with a useful life of less than one or two years. i.e., Bank Accounts, Accounts Receivable, Inventories, Prepaid Expense...
    - **Capital or Fixed Assets** – Assets with a useful life greater than one or two years and their related Depreciation Accounts when applicable. i.e., Vehicles, Equipment, Buildings, Leasehold Improvements....
    - **Other Assets** – Assets that do not fit in the Current or Capital categories.
- **2000 Liabilities** – What the business owes others
    - **Current Liabilities** – Liabilities that will be paid within one or two years. i.e., Accounts Payable, Credit Card Liability, Sales Tax Liability, Payroll Tax & Benefit Liabilities ...Current Portion of Long Term Debt.
    - **Long Term Liabilities** – Liabilities that have a pay-off period greater than one or two years. i.e., Bank Loans and Notes...
    - **Other Liabilities** – Liabilities that do not fit in the Current or Long Term Categories.
- **3000 Equity or Net Worth** – the value of the business. Assets less Liabilities.
    - **Retained Earnings** – Accumulated earnings over the life of the business
    - **Current Year Net Profit/(Loss)** – Net earnings for the current fiscal year.
    - **Owner's Equity Accounts** – This will include Owner's / Partner's investment(s); Stocks...

Account Numbers are used to keep line items in a defined sequence.

Three Essential Business Tasks

Good Bookkeeping doesn't just happen; Good Bookkeeping has to be planned

How Much Detail?

You do have some control on detail with the Balance Sheet Ledger Accounts; not much but some. For example:

- Prepaid Expense – do you need a line item for each?
- Depreciation Accounts – do you need a line item for each depreciable asset?
- Payroll Tax Liabilities – do you need a line item for each liability?

The bookkeeping software you select will help you in keeping the details to a minimum.

The Profit & Loss Report Line Items

There are not as many restrictions on what you list here as long as you keep within the basic categories (see below) you can get fairly creative. That is, you get to call the shots on naming the General Ledger Accounts. Don't let an accountant take this privilege away from you. You and your employees will use the Profit and Loss Report often to review and analyze business activity. The non-accountants on your staff need to understand what the line items represent.

Here are the basic categories for the Profit and Loss General Ledger Accounts:

- **4000 Revenue** – Monies you receive from 'Mission' based business activity.
- **5000 Direct Cost** – Disbursements tied directly to the generation of Revenue.
- **6000 Salaries, Wages, & Related Expense** – Payroll, Payroll Tax Expense, and company paid employee benefits.
- **7000 & 8000 Operating Expense** – Disbursements not tied directly to generating Revenue but needed to keep the business doors open. Overhead.

Three Essential Business Tasks

Good Bookkeeping doesn't just happen; Good Bookkeeping has to be planned

- o **Fixed Operating Expense** – Operating Expense that remain constant over a defined period of time. Contracted disbursements.
- o **Variable Operating Expense** – Operating Expenses that increase or decrease based on use.
- o **Non-cash Transactions** - Depreciation & Related Expense.
- **9000 Other Income & Expense** – Monies you receive and disburse that are not 'Mission' based. i.e., Gain/Loss on the sale of assets.

How much detail?

There is an important relationship between **Revenue and Direct Cost** that should be presented on the Profit & Loss Report. You need this information to evaluate 'Mission' based activity. Therefore, for each Revenue line item you should have a corresponding line item (multiple line items in some cases).

For example: let's say you want to be able to quickly evaluate the relationship between Revenue and Direct Cost for the sale and installation of equipment:

		Actual		Budget	
Revenue		Amount	Ratio Cost to Revenue		
4110	Equipment Sales & Installation	$ 25,000.00	100.00%	$ 25,000	100.0%
5110	Equipment Cost	$ 8,500.00	34.00%	$ 8,500	34.0%
5120	Installation Labor	$ 3,250.00	13.00%	$ 4,500	18.0%
5150	Ancillary Installation Materials	$ 1,800.00	7.20%	$ 2,200	8.8%
	Total Direct Cost	$ 13,550.00	54.20%	$ 15,200.00	60.8%

This set-up gives you a 'heads-up' in determining if the Cost to Revenue Ratio is off budget (Budgeting is discussed in *Task #3 Reliable Budgeting*); a variance indicates that you will need to examine more details to determine why.

If you only had one line for Direct Cost you would not know where to look first and may waste time chasing rabbits.

Good Bookkeeping doesn't just happen; Good Bookkeeping has to be planned

Salaries, Wages, & Related Expense

Salaries are annual pay allocated out during the year. They remain fairly constant. **Wages** are hourly pay based on the number of hours an employee works; they can vary from one pay cycle to another. If you have hourly wages you may want a line item for Overtime Wages.

The number of line items is based on how much detail you need to: ask the right questions and make informed decisions? Here is a standard set-up:

- 6011 Salaries
- 6021 Wages
- 6031 Overtime Wages
- 6111 Payroll Taxes
- 6021 Employee Benefit Exp Company Paid

How much detail do you need?

Operating Expense

As mentioned above, there are three categories of Operating Expense:

- Fixed Operating Expense;
- Variable Operating Expense;
- Non-cash Transactions.

Details here depend on what you need to see to ask the right questions and to make informed decisions. For example:

- Change in the reported Fixed Operating Expense can only happen because of: An error in posting a transaction; a change in a contract. So, 'how much detail do you need?'
- If you do a lot of printing, telephoning (minutes over contracted allocation), traveling... you may want separate line items for those Variable Operating Expenses that have high usage.

Good Bookkeeping doesn't just happen; Good Bookkeeping has to be planned

When you summarize a collection of expense in one line item do not use Miscellaneous Expense; the label doesn't tell you anything. Use Other Administrative Expense or Travel Related Expense or Telephone & Related Expense...

A good goal in creating a Functional Chart of Accounts is to limit Financial Reports (the Balance Sheet and the Profit & Loss Reports) to one page each; two pages is ok but any longer and the reports become cumbersome and will tend to create confusion among the non-accounting employees in your organization.

See *Selecting the Appropriate Bookkeeping Software* for more help in keeping your Chart of Accounts concise.

What information do you need to see on financial reports to help you?

1. ***Ask the right questions;***
2. ***Make timely informed decisions.***

3 Create a COA Lexicon - A Transaction Posting Map

Not everyone on your staff is an accountant; few probably want to be. But, employees may be assigned some financial responsibilities and, therefore, need to know how to code a transaction and how to read financial reports related to their areas of responsibility.   A Chart of Accounts Lexicon can be a big help here.

The primary purpose of the lexicon is to:

- List and define each General Ledger Account;
- Describe how to 'code' transactions that relate to the COA line items.

Creating the COA Lexicon is fairly simple; here is an example:

Good Bookkeeping doesn't just happen; Good Bookkeeping has to be planned

---

5000 – Direct Cost – *Disbursement tied directly to generating Revenue. Transactions are posted to these ledger accounts using the Payroll Item List, The Service Item List, and the Inventory Item List.*

5100 – DC Equip Install Labor – *Salaries & Wages tied directly to the installation of equipment. Payroll Tax Expense and Employee Benefit Expense are carried in Overhead (General Ledger Accounts 6000).*

Transactions are posted to this ledger account using the Payroll Timesheet Function and Install Tasks Item List. Refer to the Equipment Installation Task Code Sheet for details.

7000 – Operating Expense – *Disbursements not tied directly to generating Revenue but necessary to keep the business doors open. Overhead. Transactions are recorded using the Vendor Bill Entry Function with the Item List Function. Source Documents are coded using the following Item List Format: Transaction id + Expense Name*

Transaction ids include:
FOPE – Fixed Operating Expense
VOPE – Variable Operating Expense
SROPE – Staff Related Operating Expense
VROPE – Vehicle Related Operating Expense

Posting examples:
FOPE – Building Lease
FOPE – Business Insurance
FOPE – Telephone Internet Line Fee
VOPE – Building Utilities
VOPE – Telephone Cell Phone Excess Use Fees
VOPE – Printing Business Envelopes

Refer to 7100 - Fixed Operating Expense and 8100 Variable Operating Expense for details.

Note: Bookkeeping software Item List Functions are helpful tools to gaining and maintaining 'good bookkeeping'. Refer to #4 Selecting Bookkeeping Software.

If you want to gain and maintain Good Bookkeeping you need to make sure employees have a resource to help them assign financial transactions to the appropriate General Ledger Account and help them

Good Bookkeeping doesn't just happen; Good Bookkeeping has to be planned

read and understand financial reports. A Chart of Accounts Lexicon is the resource.

4 Select the appropriate Bookkeeping Software

You have a whole lot of choices here so here are a few recommendations to help you in your selecting:

- Know what you need before selecting. Take time to describe what you want from the Bookkeeping Software before you go looking. Review a number of software providers on the internet to get an idea of the functions available.
- Don't be swayed by all the bells and whistles. Bells and whistles are great but make sure they do not cost too much to use. Is the time and effort put into getting that fancy report cost effective?
- Be alert to the term 'easy'. Bookkeeping is not easy nor is it easy to set-up Good Bookkeeping. It takes time and thought.
- Select software that will allow you to use your own Chart of Accounts. Why should you have to redo financial reports in a spread sheet to meet your needs? Downloading and manipulating financial data can only lead to problems.
- Select software that has an Item List function. This will allow you to define and schedule recurring transactions; help you maintain uniform descriptions for transactions; and help you limit the number of General Ledger Accounts on your Chart of Accounts.
- Select software that reports Functions or Departments in parallel columns. This will allow you to use the same Ledger Accounts for each Function or Department.
- If you are going to have a payroll, make sure there is an integrated payroll function in the software package. You don't want to be making journal entries.
- Make sure that up-grades to the software will allow you to keep your current database and Chart of Accounts. You don't want to have to reinvent the wheel when you up-grade the software.
- Always purchase software that goes beyond your need. You never know when you will need more functions.

Good Bookkeeping doesn't just happen; Good Bookkeeping has to be planned

- Look for software that has good tech support (local is best). "Nothing ever works right" is a constant you can count on.

Don't rush into a purchase. It will cost you more to straighten out than the cost of patience.

Why did you select the Bookkeeping Software you currently have?

What do you want from / need from your bookkeeping software?

5 Define the Software Functions you will use

Bookkeepers are notorious at devising their own approach to using bookkeeping software functions. But, 'what happens when the bookkeeper needs time off, quits, is fired?'

Here is what will happen if you have not defined how the Software Functions are used in your business:

- The new bookkeeper or temporary bookkeeper will attempt to follow the previous bookkeeper's approach but will more than likely implement their approach to recording transactions;
- You will lose the uniform characteristic of good bookkeeping for sure. You may lose the other characteristics also.
- If you attempt to do the task yourself you are going to make errors that may take some time to straighten out.

Create a Bookkeeping Software Lexicon to gain reasonable assurance that you will maintain good bookkeeping even when the bookkeeper needs time off. Here is an example:

Other Item Function – Allows you to define a transaction and assign the transaction to a General Ledger Account. Helps you maintain a uniform set of entries in your financial database especially for recurring transactions; speeds up data entry. Used to record

Good Bookkeeping doesn't just happen; Good Bookkeeping has to be planned

Operating Expense. Each transaction is preceded by an id and then a one to four word description.

Transaction ids:
- FOPE – Fixed Operating Expense
- VOPE – Variable Operating Expense
- SRE – Staff Related Operating Expense
- VEH – Vehicle Related Operating Expense

Examples:
- FOPE – Telephone Cell Phone Contracted Exp
- VOPE – Telephone Cell Phone Excess Use Exp
- SRE – Staff Travel Meals
- SRE – Gas Mileage Reimbursement
- VEH – Vehicle Fuel Expense
- VEH – Vehicle Maintenance

A Software Lexicon will help you communicate to your bookkeeper just how you want them to use the bookkeeping software to maintain good bookkeeping. The fact that you have a Bookkeeping Software Lexicon should be included in the Bookkeeper's Job Description.

6 Write Internal Financial Controls

Bookkeepers are told what to do; bookkeepers do not make decisions on their own

That is an unsettling quote for most bookkeepers. We (I include myself because I've been a bookkeeper) tend to think we are expected to know what to do without being told. After all, we were hired because we possess the knowledge and skill to complete the task. But being qualified has nothing to do with the point of the quote.

Bookkeepers are vulnerable to accusations of misappropriating company assets; they have also been known to misappropriate funds. You cannot avoid this 100% but you can provide reasonable assurance that accusation about and actual fraud won't happen by writing Internal Financial Controls.

Three Essential Business Tasks

Good Bookkeeping doesn't just happen; Good Bookkeeping has to be planned

Internal Financial Controls are written 'rules' that inform the bookkeeper and other employees what they can and cannot do in relation to the financial assets of the business. It is not a matter of trust but one of protecting the backside of the bookkeeper (other employees also) and the assets of the business.

When writing Internal Financial Controls apply the KISS principle — *Keep it simple not stupendous.* You want to communicate not impress; you want the part time high school student in the warehouse or office and the CEO to be able to implement the control. By the way, you will have more trouble with the CEO then the part time student.

IFC's for the bookkeeper will among other things:

- Address the limitations of the bookkeeper.
- Identify who has authority to initiate and to approve financial transactions — both sales and disbursements. This should include levels of authority to approve transactions. **Not the Bookkeeper**.
- Define how transactions are initiated and source documents that are needed to finalize the transaction.
- Define how company assets can be used. i.e., Company Vehicles, Employee Expense Reimbursements, Company Credit Cards, Petty Cash, Cell Phones...
- Provide timelines for submitting source documents for processing and penalties for not submitting timely and accurate documentation.
- Define information flow — who gets what when and in what format.

Internal Financial Controls are not legal documents; therefore, they can be formal or informal. The only requirement is that there is a place on the document that indicates that the business owner has approved the IFC.

Three Essential Business Tasks

Good Bookkeeping doesn't just happen; Good Bookkeeping has to be planned

IFC 005.011 – Company Credit Cards are issued to Department Managers to allow them to purchase supplies needed to support their department operations. All charges must be supported by a receipt initialed by the manager and coded to the appropriate project, when applicable, and expense category. Receipts are due no later than one week after purchase. Unsupported transactions will be charged back to the manager. Credit Cards are not to be used for personal or un-approved purchases as defined in IFC 005.321. Abuse of Credit Card use can lead to termination.

Approved by: _____ on: _____

Xyz Company - Financial Control Manual

Policy Number & Title: #001.011 – Using Company Credit Card

Distribution: Company wide

Rational or Purpose Statement: To reduce the cost of payable processing and to ensure that employees understand how to use the card.

Policy Statement:

- Company xyz Credit Cards are issued to all department managers to use in conducting business and to make the purchasing of products and services needed to carry out their responsibilities simpler.
- All charges must be supported by Vendor Invoices coded to projects and describing product or service received if not obvious on the support documents. Invoices must be initialed in the lower right corner by the originator and the person approving the transaction.
- Travel expense source documents must indicate reason for travel and if meals who was present. Overnight travel must be pre-approved using the 'Travel Agenda Notice' as noted in Financial Policy 005.21.
- Charges greater than the approval level of a manager must be approved by the CFO or CEO.
- All source documents must be in the accounting office with-in one week of activity.
- Un-supported charges will be charged to the manager through the payroll system if support documents are not received in a timely manner – with-in two weeks of the Credit Card Statement (10th of each month).
- Credit cards are not to be used for personal expense or cash advances. Abuse of Credit Card use will mean termination of Credit Card privileges and could lead to termination of employment.

Date of last review: _____ **Approved by:** _____

Financial Control #005.011 – Using Company Credit Card

Good Bookkeeping doesn't just happen; Good Bookkeeping has to be planned

When to write IFC's?

Before you start your business; before you hire a bookkeeper. These are the ideal times. But there is no time like the present. Even if you are running a solo operation, begin to prepare for when you will hire a bookkeeper or use a bookkeeping service.

If you are a bookkeeper and do not have IFC's on file, begin writing them and get them approved. You need some protection; your boss needs some protection when you need to take time off.

7 Write Bookkeeping Procedures

'Best Practices' is a phrase often used to describe procedures. Bookkeeping Procedures define the best practices you have selected to gain and maintain an efficient, effective, functional, and uniform financial record keeping process for your business.

If you do not provide your bookkeeper with written Bookkeeping Procedures they are going to complete their assigned task their way which will become your way. Getting them to change can be very difficult.

But, "What happens when your bookkeeper needs time off?"

A temporary will attempt to follow your bookkeeper's approach but will more than likely implement their approach. If you attempt as the business owner to complete the task in the interim, you are going to make errors that may take some time to correct.

The best way to avoid losing Good Bookkeeping is to have written Bookkeeping Procedures in place.

Like IFC's, Bookkeeping Procedures are a means to communicate and not impress, so keep the KISS principle in mind when writing. Well written procedures will allow a new or temporary bookkeeper to become

Good Bookkeeping doesn't just happen; Good Bookkeeping has to be planned

productive in a short period of time; they will also allow other employees to help the bookkeeper during peak periods.

Do not let the simplicity of a task convince you that a procedure is not merited. The simplest task performed incorrectly can cause problems down the line.

Bookkeeping Procedures do not replace the bookkeeper; they provide reasonable assurance that financial recording keeping will be efficient, effective, functional, and uniform even when the bookkeeper needs time off.

Two examples:

---

xyz Company – Bookkeeping Procedure
#050.001 Receiving Vendor Invoices

Purpose statement – to speed up verifying and processing vendor invoices.
Software Function – None applicable.
Prerequisites – None
Procedure – Vendor invoices are received by the Receptionist;
- Open and collate the invoices;
- Highlight in yellow the Date, Invoice Number, Purchase Order Number, the Project, and the total amount.
- File the highlighted Vendor Invoices in the 'to be posted' alpha sorter.
- Deliver the 'to be posted' alpha sorter to the bookkeeper daily.

Note: Vendor Invoices are to go from the Receptionist to the Bookkeeper only. If other employees need to see an invoice they can go to the bookkeeper and request the information. IFC 50.100

Date of last review: _____Approved by: _____

The above is a very simple procedure but an important one when processing source documents. Highlighting important information is the first step in verifying information and in speeding up processing.

Good Bookkeeping doesn't just happen; Good Bookkeeping has to be planned

xyz Company – Bookkeeping Procedure
#050.013 Recording Vendor Invoices

Purpose statement – to ensure timely and uniform recording of charges.

Software Function – Vendor Bill Entry Function; Item List Function.

Prerequisites – Working knowledge of the Enter Bill Function and the Item List Function of x software. Vendor Invoice has been received, verified, approved, and filed in the posting sorter.

Procedure – All transactions are recorded by Vendor Invoice when received.

- Verify that the Vendor Invoice has been properly highlighted, approved, and coded.
- Open the Vendor Bill Entry Software Function.
- Select the Vendor; new vendor, refer to Procedure 050.011
- Post the Date, Invoice Number, and Payment Schedule (10th or 25th - See IFC 050.210 for details).
- Record charges using Item List Code and Project List. One line for each item/project.
- Reconcile Total posted to source document.
- Mark the Vendor Invoice Posted in the lower right corner with your initials. "Posted by…"
- File the Vendor Invoice in the 'to be paid' alpha sorter.

Date of last Review: _____ Approved By: _____

Procedures Bookkeeping #050.013 Recording Vendor Invoices

Bookkeeping Procedures provide the framework for Good Bookkeeping. They will not replace the bookkeeper but will give you reasonable assurance that you will have an efficient, an effective, a Functional, and a Uniform set of books even when the bookkeeper needs time off.

Basic Bookkeeping Procedures you should have in place:

- Receiving Source Documents for receipts and disbursements;
- Recording Sales;
- Recording Disbursements;
- Printing Checks
- Depositing Receipts
- Bank Reconciliations

Good Bookkeeping doesn't just happen; Good Bookkeeping has to be planned

8 Support your Bookkeeper

Your bookkeeper needs feedback to help them become an efficient, effective, flexible, reliable employee. Annual evaluations work (somewhat), but frequent feedback is more beneficial.

Ten, Twenty, Thirty Minutes

Just setting down with the bookkeeper weekly for a few minutes and asking how things are going is the first format for feedback.

This short period of time will allow the employee to talk about what they are doing and any issues they need assistance in resolving. It creates a proactive approach to catching any problems before they hatch into bigger issues. It also gives you the opportunity to: praise, comment, educate, encourage, and thank them.

Twenty to thirty minutes a week can produce a hundred fold in return.

If you decide to use this approach, schedule a weekly time with your bookkeeper and keep to the schedule. If you find yourself missing or re-scheduling these short meetings, you may be implying that your bookkeeper isn't that important. Bad move.

Self-Evaluation

A more formal approach is to develop a self-evaluation form for the employee to complete at least monthly and forward to you or their immediate manager.

Scheduled self-evaluation encourages the employee to take time to look at what they are doing and determine if they are meeting their own expectation as well as those of their employer.

Good Bookkeeping doesn't just happen; Good Bookkeeping has to be planned

Self-evaluation gives the employee the opportunity to resolve or ask for help in resolving any issues early. Self-evaluation also takes the sting out of annual performance reviews.

The self-evaluation form should include:

- A list of performance criteria you have established with the employee;
- A scoring scheme. i.e., 1 low → 5 high
- Space for the employee to comment on their scoring
- Space for the employee's supervisor to comment
- Space for the employee to list goals for the next evaluation period
- Space to comment on progress toward reaching goals

Comments should include issues that are preventing the employee from meeting expectations and goals as well as situations that are helping the employee move forward.

If you are going to use Self Evaluation, be sure to read them and respond in a timely manner. Don't use the excuse that you are too busy; if you do, you will pay for it sometime later.

Formal Evaluation

Your formal evaluation scheme should be stated in the employees' Job Description. If you change your annual evaluation approach, give your employee enough notice so that they will not be surprised.

Rehire the employee after their annual evaluation with a new or up-dated Job Description. This gives you the opportunity to up-date company history; re-define the position; and add to or adjust responsibilities and outcomes.

Supporting and evaluating are really one in the same activity. If you take the time in advance to speak with your bookkeeper you are going to have a more productive employee.

Good Bookkeeping doesn't just happen; Good Bookkeeping has to be planned

9 Provide Skill Development Opportunities

Enroll your bookkeeper in The American Institute of Professional Bookkeepers (AIPB). You can find them on the internet www.aipb.org . They offer a monthly newsletter that presents current issues in business recordkeeping, bookkeeping tips, as well as skill development opportunities.

What are you doing to support your bookkeeper? Make a list of ways you could improve the support. Then put the list to work.

10 Create a Bookkeeper's Notebook

A Bookkeeper's Notebook is a resource that will: help you maintain good bookkeeping even when your bookkeeper needs time off; enable a temporary or new bookkeeper to become productive in the shortest amount of time; place all the information a bookkeeper needs in one place.

Information in the notebook should include:

- Mission Statement
- Current Company Operating Plan. For details go to *Task #2 Timely Planning.*
- Company Organization Chart and the Bookkeeper's Job Description
- Business Information list
- Chart of Accounts and the Chart of Accounts Lexicon
- Bookkeeping Software Information and the Software Function Lexicon
- Internal Financial Controls
- Bookkeeping Procedures
- Current Operating Budget. For details go to *Task #3 Reliable Budgeting*
- Self-Evaluation Forms

Good Bookkeeping doesn't just happen; Good Bookkeeping has to be planned

How to avoid financial abuse

Bookkeepers are told what to do; they do not make decisions on their own.

It's not a matter of not knowing what to do or trust, but a matter of covering the bookkeeper's back side and protecting business assets for the business owner. Internal Financial Controls inform the bookkeeper what they can do and Bookkeeping Procedures inform the bookkeeper how to complete tasks. But there is still a gap to gaining and maintaining reasonable assurance that business assets are secure; that financial assets are secure.

The Problem with the Separation of Duties Principle

Auditors love to write up businesses for not adhering to the principle of, "Separation of Duties". What this means is that a person posting transactions should not be the same person writing checks – have access to checks; a person billing customers should not be the same person who receives customer payments; and so on. Securing company assets and preventing fraud are the motivation behind this principle.

Separation of duties is a great principle but if a business wants to make a profit; if a not-for-profit wants a low overhead percent, it is impractical. One bookkeeper is enough overhead expense for a small business.

The way around the 'Separation of duties' principal includes written Internal Financial Controls, written Bookkeeping Procedures, and a Financial Review Process in place. We have covered the first two. Here are a few recommendations of a Financial Review Process.

Good Bookkeeping doesn't just happen; Good Bookkeeping has to be planned

Financial Review Process

You can assign financial responsibility but you cannot as a business owner relinquish financial responsibility. The buck always stops with the boss whether they like it or not.

You will never get to 100% assurance that your financial assets are secure but you can get fairly close if you will take the time to review financial reports. There is no assumption here that your bookkeeper is a crook or any employee for that matter, but you need to make sure that there are no doors or windows open that could allow someone to be tempted to misappropriate company assets.

Here is a basic list of information you should review at regular intervals:

- Vendor and Customer activity – you should know who you are doing business with and have a general idea of the volume of business. Make sure you have a process in place to approve vendors and customers.
- Bank Statements and Bank Reconciliations – if anything is going south you will be able to detect it by a focused review of Bank Statements and Bank Reconciliation Reports. Here are a few things to look for:
  - Check numbers out of sequence
  - Deposit Adjustments
  - Check Signature
  - Vendors
- Select Vendors and Customers at random and verify the support documentation.
- Payroll Reports – Look for variance in Gross Wages.
- Weekly Deposit Report
- Weekly Disbursement Report
- Weekly Sales by Product and/or Service
- Budget Variance Reports – Monthly and Year to Date

Other things you should do:

Good Bookkeeping doesn't just happen; Good Bookkeeping has to be planned

- Make sure that all payment vouchers you sign or authorize have the appropriate approved support documentation.
- Make sure that all sales are supported by approved support documents.
- Be able to print financial reports on your own.

Create a list of items that you will review at regular intervals. Schedule the review time. Stick to the schedule. It is your money.

Good Bookkeeping Summary

Bookkeeping is overhead. Bookkeepers are often seen as important but a necessary evil; reviled by some staff because of their 'gate keeper' status. They, therefore, need the support and recognition of the business owner and adequate resources to complete their task.

Bookkeepers are not clairvoyant; they do not know when information is needed automatically or how _you_ want information recorded and reported. They can assume but their assumption will not necessarily meet your needs.

One thing a bookkeeper learns quickly is that their time is not 'their time'. It is controlled by the needs of others with-in the company as well as customers, vendors, and government agencies. "I can get it done on...." is not necessarily a valid response for a bookkeeper.

Adequate software, a well thought out Chart of Accounts, Written Internal Financial Controls and Bookkeeping Procedures are the basics to enable a bookkeeper to help you gain and maintain good bookkeeping. It is up to the business owner to provide the basics and more.

Task #2 Timely Planning

Task #2 Timely Planning – is next. "In planning for battle I have always found that plans are useless, but planning is indispensable". A quote from General Dwight David Eisenhower that captures the essence of this task. Timely Planning includes evaluating where you are in relation to where you want to be; then writing or refining goals and related tactics to address the challenges you uncover along the way.

One of the frequent errors many small business owners make is assuming that planning is a onetime activity or an annual activity. The point of origin of this assumption surprisingly comes from business books, blogs, and consultants.

This assumption is true if business is a one-time activity or a once a year activity. But, if business is an ongoing activity then business planning is an ongoing activity.

My recommendations to active planning:

1. Identifying Change
2. Choosing an approach to planning
3. Avoiding a common error in planning
4. Moving from a Start-up to a Business Operating Plan

1 Identifying Change

You can ignore change but you cannot ignore the effect change has on how you plan to do business and how you do business.

There is one constant that you can always rely on in business – *Change*. You can ignore it and suffer the consequence or you can identify it and either embrace it or curtail its effect by timely planning.

You can identify and define change by studying your Business Environment and by evaluating where you are in your Business Cycle.

Your Business Environment

A Business Environment is the sum of what is taking place inside and around your business; internal and external factors (for lack of a better word) that are having, may have, or will have in the near or distance future a direct effect on what you do and how you do it.

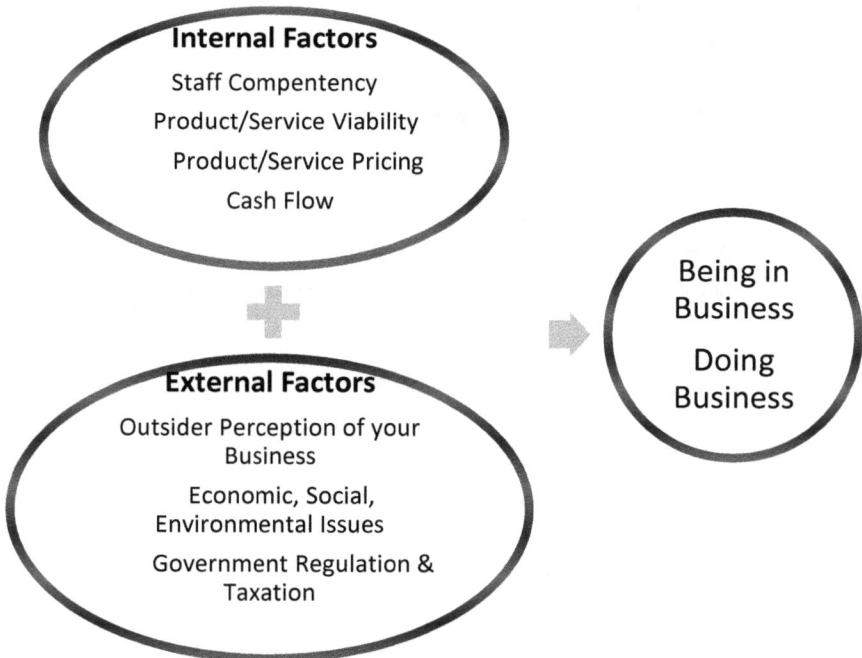

Internal Factors
Staff Compentency
Product/Service Viability
Product/Service Pricing
Cash Flow

External Factors
Outsider Perception of your Business

Economic, Social, Environmental Issues

Government Regulation & Taxation

Being in Business

Doing Business

Three Essential Business Tasks
If business is an ongoing activity then planning is an ongoing activity

Internal factors are those things that you usually have control over; **External factors** may be under your control but are usually outside of your purview of influence.

Identifying, defining, and implementing goals and related tactics to address the challenges each of these factors present is critical to maintaining a reasonable assurance of success in your business venture.

Negative or positive effect is not the issue; promoting the positive and curtailing the effect of the negative with written goals and tactics is.

What are the internal and external factors that are having or that may have an effect on what you do and how you do it? What can you do to promote the positive factors; curtail the negative factors?

Your Business Cycle
A Business Cycle usually has five reference points and is presented in a circular diagram like the following:

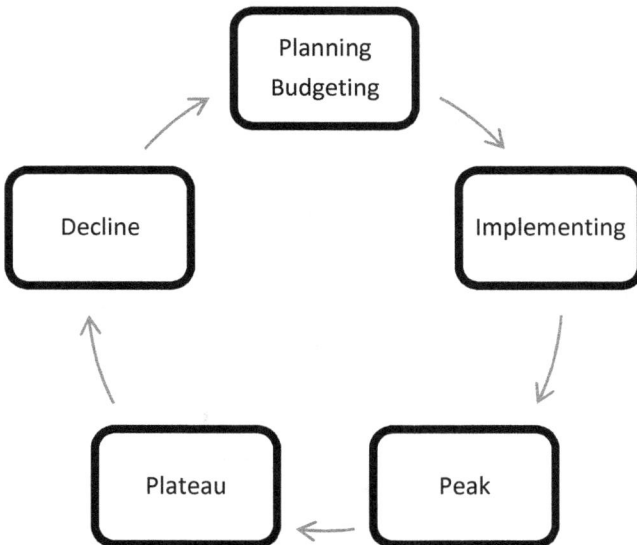

Three Essential Business Tasks
If business is an ongoing activity then planning is an ongoing activity

The goal in business is to stay just above the Peak point in the cycle. Peak, Plateau, and Decline can mean among other things:

- You have reached your capacity to generate business and any attempt to go beyond may be detrimental (we will get into this when discussing budgeting).
- Public interest has diminished or may be diminishing.

Pinpointing your position and the direction you are moving in the cycle will give you a 'heads up' on change that may be taking place in the business environment; an early warning that you may need to do some re-planning.

Where are you in your Business Cycle? Can you define why you are there?

It is not the strongest of the species that survive, or the most intelligent, but the one most responsive to change. Charles Darwin

2 Choosing an approach to planning
- Inactive Planning
- Re-active Planning
- Pre-active Planning
- Proactive Planning

Inactive Planning & Reactive Planning

Many, far too many, entrepreneurs are inactive and reactive planners. **The inactive planner** just sits and waits for business to come to them and tends to blame others when they fail.

The reactive planner starts a sale because the business up the street has a sale; acts before completing the due diligence needed to determine if the 'sale' will actually improve business.

Both inactive and reactive planners will often say, "I have a business plan; dust it off; and then say, 'why isn't it working?'"

Pre-active Planning

The Pre-active Planner attempts to predict what will take place and then plan around the prediction. It is very difficult to predict the future even more difficult to predict the outcome of the future.

Pre-active planning is often reading tea leaves, listening to and accepting unconfirmed advice, or following trends that are really fads.

The best a Pre-active Planner can do is guess then hope that he has guessed right.

Proactive Planning

The Proactive Planner plans for the future by reviewing the past and refining the way he identifies and addresses change so that he is ready for the challenges an ever-changing business environment may present.

Proactive planning is a 'what if' approach to moving a business forward; "I am doing this now but what if I do this or have to do this?"

If your goal is to have reasonable assurance of business success, which approach to planning would you choose?

3 Avoiding a common error in planning

A big mistake made in business planning is to plan for only one eventuality. Two of the best examples of this are in the Technology Crash of 1999/2001 and the home building/housing crash of 2007/08.

During the lead-up to each of these economic down turns, businesses (and individuals) were focused more on making money then sustaining a business. Entrepreneurs were stumbling over each other to get a piece of the action. Companies were being bought and sold right and left. Find your 'niche' was the operative planning approach; the narrower your missions focus the more money you could make.

Three Essential Business Tasks
If business is an ongoing activity then planning is an ongoing activity

- A plumber found that he could make more money working as a sub-contractor to a builder than servicing established home owners.
- Dot.com ventures relied on their product advancement without recognizing the effect of competition.
- Corporations were spending capital racing to corner the market but critical cash flow issues were left for a another time.

Businesses gave up sustainable income for more money in the short-run, work that seemed to have no end, or spending before realizing a profit. Then the crash.

Hundreds of businesses were turned up-side-down. They were scrambling to get paid for work done and at the same time trying to get more work, ignoring the obvious. They were typical Inactive, Reactive, Pre-active Planners. Smart people with faulty vision.

What could have changed the outcome for many of these businesses was a Proactive approach to planning – anticipating the **possibility** of a change in their business environment and preparing a plan to address the change – A what if plan.

What happened was that very few businesses looked at the future with change in mind. They tended to stay in the present as if it would never change. "I'll just keep going; doing what I do and I'll be fine."

Take a look at where you are in your business planning. Is your focus too narrow?

Unless you include the possibility of change in your planning, you are ignoring the reality of being in business and doing business.

"What if I have to do "X"? Is a valuable question for gaining and maintaining a reasonable assurance of success in business?

4 Moving from the Start-up to an Operating Plan

There are two distinct stages to business planning. The first is the Business Start-up Plan; the second is the Business Operating Plan. Movement from the first to the second is an important step to gaining and maintaining a reasonable assurance of succeeding in business.

The Start-up Business Plan

Most entrepreneurs remember their Business Start-up Plan. Not the content necessarily but the arduous process of creating the document. It takes time and if you use an outside source to assist you, it can be expensive.

If someone were to suggest that you need to re-do your Business Plan periodically, you would probable say, "Really?" Then ignore their advice and go about your business the best you can.

Just a note: I am not recommending you rewrite your Business Plan.

The primary purpose of a Business Start-up Plan is twofold: the first is to persuade others – investors, bankers, potential partners, vendors – to join you in the business venture; the second is obvious, to guide you through the business start-up process.

Once you have persuaded and initiated the business, the Start-up Plan quickly becomes less relevant. Some find it hard to accept this position. Let me explain:

> *Did you follow your Business Start-up Plan to the letter? Or, did you find that some of your ideas worked, some ideas did not work, and some ideas needed to be tweaked to work? And as time progressed, did you find that you had to adopt different strategies to address the needs and changes in your business environment?*

Every time you eliminated an idea, changed an idea, added an idea to your original business plan, you made the original less and less relevant. You were actually re-planning your business each time you made a change.

Re-planning is not a matter of writing a new Business Plan – unless you are refocusing your whole operation. Re-planning is moving from the start-up stage to the operational stage; then keeping the Operating Plan current.

The Business Operating Plan

A Business Operating Plan is an internal document used to communicate to employees and other stakeholders how the business will address the challenges presented by changes in the business environment. It is a *succinct* restatement of Mission, Vision, Core Values, and Strategy.

When to prepare

Some, really very few businesses are able to postpone the process, completing the task annually. Most businesses should schedule a review at least monthly and refine the current plan as the need arises. Some businesses may even need to keep a close eye on things weekly.

Change is the key. When you detect a change in the business environment that is or that may have an effect on your business venture, it's time to refine the Operating Plan; to create a 'what if' plan just in case or to address actual changes.

How to prepare

- Identify, define, & evaluate change(s)
- Write goals and related tactics to address change(s)

Three Essential Business Tasks
If business is an ongoing activity then planning is an ongoing activity

Identify, define, and evaluate change

There are two sets of change you will need to identify, define, and evaluate in your business environment:

- Internal Change
- External Change

Three key questions:

- What is happening inside and outside my business that may affect my being in business and how I do business?
- How will it affect operations?
- How am I going to adapt?

Here are a few examples:

- New Technology (define) will / may cause…; and require…
- New product line (define) will / may cause…; and require…
- New competitor (define) will / may cause…; and require…
- Additional staff (define) will / may cause…; and require…
- New government regulations (define) will / may cause…; and require…

Write goals and related tactics to address change

For each change you identify, define, and evaluate, write goals and related tactics that address the challenge of dealing with the change. Goals and Tactics should start with an active verb and include a measurable component or outcome. A Goal is the end result of the action (Tactics) you will take.

Employees will use the Goals and Tactics you present here to guide them in producing the outcome(s) you are looking for.

Here is an example:

- **Change** –Competition is beginning to make inroads into our customer base because we are often unable to meet the demand.

- **Goal** – Increase billable time of Service Technicians by 5 hours a week.
- **Related Tactic** - hire an administrative support employee to coordinate service calls and to complete paperwork.

Keeping the Operating Plan Current

There are four sections to the Business Operating Plan I am recommending:

1   Mission – History, Purpose, Future
2   Vision – Internal and External perceptions
3   Core Values – Operational Ethics
4   Strategy – How you will address change

To ensure that information in each section is current, correct, and usable, perform a review at regular intervals. Employees will use the information you communicate through the Operating Plan to initiate activity that will help them provide the outcomes you are anticipating.

Gathering information

Use Questions. I have included a starter list of questions below. You may need to add to, delete, or modify the questions to fit your business. Write each question on the top of a separate sheet of paper; then brainstorm a response. Some of your best answers will come from employees, customers, and vendors. Don't hesitate to involve them in the gathering of information.

Questions are how we discover. Use them often; use them wisely.

History – Future – Purpose

- When was your business started? How many years in business?
- How many employees did you start the business with? How many do you have now?
- List three things (goals if you wish) you have accomplished: In the last three months; six months; twelve months; two years; three years.

Three Essential Business Tasks
If business is an ongoing activity then planning is an ongoing activity

- List three things you want to accomplish: In the next three months; six months; twelve months; two years; three years.
- What is the purpose of your business venture? Start the statement with an active verb. i.e., provide, enlist, repair…

Vision & Core Values

- What do you want people seeing, hearing, feeling, talking about when they: See your business name; Hear your business name; Call your business; Have talked with others about your business; Have experienced your business service or product?
- What are people seeing, hearing, feeling, talking about when they: See your business name; hear your business name; Call your business; have talked with others about your business; have experienced your business service or product?

Strategy

- What changes have you noticed / are you noticing in your business environment that are having / may have an effect on your ability to do business as planned?
- How will / are these changes affecting your business?
- How are you responding to / do you plan to respond to these changes? What can happen if you ignore the changes and do nothing?
- What changes in your business environment do you anticipate in the future that will affect your ability to do business as planned? How will these changes affect your business plans? How are you preparing to respond to these future changes? What may happen if you don't prepare?
- List three to five things that are interfering with your ability to carry out your business plans. What are your plans for dealing with these issues? What may happen if you do not make and initiate plans to deal with these issues?
- List three to five things that are helping you achieve your business goals. Are they applicable to the future? If yes, how do you plan to keep them active? If no, how do you plan to faze them out?

Writing the Business Operating Plan

Content for the Operating Plan will originate from your response to the questions. The final Operating Plan should be no longer than four pages. Short is good. Here is the outline and a few examples:

Mission – History, Purpose, Future

- History – Write a succinct paragraph describing where, when and how the business was started and what has been accomplished.
- Purpose – Write a succinct sentence defining what you do.
- Future – Write a succinct paragraph describing where the business is heading.

You want employees to be able to describe your business in one minute or less. You want everyone on the same page when they tell others what the business is about.

Don't be afraid to include mistakes in this statement. Employees and other stakeholders as well as customers already know when the business has made a wrong turn. Attempting to hide the fact will only make employees and others lose confidence in your leadership. Communicate how you are attempting to turn the business around.

Example:

Started in 1989, xyz Company has for the past eighteen years developed the reputation for (what you do)...by (how you do it).... In 2001 we changed our focus to ... in order to take advantage of the expansion in the building market. In 2007 we had to re-focus on ... because of the building market crash.

Known for ... xyz Company (Active verb. i.e., provides, coordinates, collects) ....

In the next three years we plan to do... to enable xyz Company to .... Next year we will ....

Three Essential Business Tasks
If business is an ongoing activity then planning is an ongoing activity

Don't be afraid to tweak your Purpose Statement. Your purpose as a business is not based on what you want to do but a combination of what you can do and what customers need. ***Be open to change and you will be able to have reasonable assurance of success.***

Each time you do a review of your business you need to re-write History, Purpose, and Future. This may seem like a lot of repetitive writing but the process will help you:

- Refresh your experience as an entrepreneur;
- Note how you have moved the business idea;
- Keep employees informed. There is nothing worse than misinformed employees. Rumors can kill a business.

When things seem to be going wrong, review your history.

- Highlight the achievements and celebrate;
- Highlight the missteps and make note of what went wrong and what you 'could of, should of, would of' will do to overcome.
- Address the change in your Business Operating Plan.

Vision

Vision should include both an atmosphere you want to create within your business and response you are looking for from employees, customers, your community, vendors… when they see your business name, hear your business name, when they talk about your business. The impact you want to have on customers, your community, your vendors, your employees. Vision and Core Values are closely linked; a response to vision may be the effect of a Core Value.

- A working environment where employees are united with single purpose influencing customers to spread the word that xyz Company is the place to go for….
- Friendly; Fair; Knowledgeable.

Three Essential Business Tasks
If business is an ongoing activity then planning is an ongoing activity

Core Values

Core Values reflect the ethics of your business; how you treat and respond to employees, customers, vendors, the environment, the community. This can be a bulleted list or a descriptive sentence or paragraph.

- Treat employees with respect; avoid embarrassing them in front of peers, customers, and vendors.
- Give customers the right to spout off without retaliation; focusing on resolving the issues.
- Accept 'no I can't' as a valid response so as not to force an employee, customer, or vendor into a compromising position.

Strategy

Here is where the rubber meets the road. Strategy will include a list of goals and related tactics you will use to address change in your business environment and give direction to your employees to help them complete their responsibilities and move the business forward.

Goals and Tactics should start with an active verb and include a measurable component or outcome.

- **Goal** – Increase revenue by 3% each quarter for the fiscal year beginning July 1, 2010 while maintaining the current average Net Profit Margin of 8%.
- **Related Tactic** - Increase billable time of Service Technicians by 5 hours a week by hiring an administrative support employee to coordinate service calls and complete paperwork.

Strategy Focus

There are at least four areas for strategy consideration:

1. Administrative – general business management;
2. Production – providing service and product;
3. Marketing – promoting the business;

4   Sales – contracting the purchase of service and product.

Strategy focus may include:

- Obstacles you need to remove or decrease their impact;
- Skills employees need to acquire;
- Attitudes that need to change – Internal and External;
- Assets, New Employees, Technology … you need to acquire;
- Budgets you need to construct.

History, Future, and Strategy will change more frequently than Purpose, Vision, and Core Values. But do not skip Purpose, Vision, and Core Values when you set out to refine your Business Operating Plan. Just reorganizing and rewriting the content can help employees refocus and improve productivity.

Timely Planning Summary

Change is a constant you can rely on in business. You can ignore it but you can't ignore the effect change will or may have on what you do and how you do it.

Become a Proactive Business Planner and you will be able to gain and maintain reasonable assurance of succeeding.

Here are two quotes that speak directly to Timely Planning:

It is not the strongest of the species that survive, or the most intelligent, but the one most responsive to change. Charles Darwin

In preparing for battle I have always found that plans are useless, but planning is indispensable. General Dwight D Eisenhower

The only secret to success in business is working smart; doing the right things at the appropriate time correctly.   Timely Planning is one of the right things.

Three Essential Business Tasks

If business is an ongoing activity then planning is an ongoing activity

Task #3 Reliable Budgeting

Task #3 Reliable Budgeting – is the third task. Before you can complete a timely and reliable budget you need Task #1 Good Bookkeeping & Task #2 Timely Planning in place.

In setting up your financial record keeping you establish line items for financially significant numbers you will use to evaluate business activity – budget line items.

During planning you profile the numbers to get a handle on what it cost to be in business and what it cost to do business. These two sets of numbers make up your Business Operating Budget.

An Operating Budget is your Business Plans presented in financial terms.

Here is a task that is usually on the top of the 'put off to a later date' list. 'We know we shouldn't but budgeting has never really been a help.' is the reasoning. When the task is completed it is usually at the last minute and the numbers aren't that reliable. And that is what takes us back to, 'budgeting has never really been a help.' reasoning.

Here are three recommendations to help resolve this circular dilemma.

1   Determine why you are going to create a budget;
2   Set a process in place that will give you reliable numbers;
3   Use an Operating Budget Formula

1 Determine why you are going to create a budget

Budgets are created for a variety of reasons. Here are three of the more common:

1   **Control or limit spending** – restrain or stop spending at a certain level;
2   **Evaluate Spending** – determine the reason for the variance in spending; is it a trend or a temporary situation? Then project future spending according to the finding;
3   **Control when necessary and Evaluate** - There comes a time when you have to decide on the Cost/Benefit ratio of an activity. You don't want to limit spending on the activity right away because there is benefit potential; but, there will come a time when the cost may exceed the benefit and you will need to set a limit on how much you can allocate to the activity.

The follow-up question to either approach is, "What affect will the 'reasoning' have on your ability to be in business and your ability to do business in an ever changing business environment?"

With the above in mind, write a reason you will use to support your budgeting tasks.

2 How to ensure reliable numbers

The standard approach to budgeting is to start collecting information three to four months before the budget is due. The negative to this approach is that the information you collect is 'old' by the time the budget rolls out. Here is our question again, "What affect will this approach have on your being in business and doing business in an ever changing Business Environment?"

If business is a onetime event, then budgeting is a onetime activity. But, if business is an ongoing event, then budgeting is an ongoing activity.

Three Essential Business Tasks
A budget is your Operating Plan stated in financial terms

'An ongoing activity' means that budgeting is part of your weekly and monthly routine; time set aside to:

- Review and analyze what you are doing against what you have planned to do;
- Note the effect;
- Write or refine goals and related tactics to curtail the negative and amplify the positive.
- Profile budget changes
- Post budget changes

Budgeting always follows planning; budgeting without a plan is like spiting in the wind; you won't like the return. Every time you review and refine your Business Operating Plan to address change you should review and refine (when necessary) your budget because change has a rippling effect. But, be aware of these two factors:

- **Trends** – Trends tend to have a permanent effect. Therefore, when you note a trend in Cost or Expense you should make a change in your budget and allow it to ripple through the budget cycle and into future budgets until it changes again.
- **Fads** – Fads tend to be temporary and may fluctuate from one cycle to another. Fads can become trends but should not be noted in the budget until you are reasonably sure they will remain.

Monthly budget reviews will actually take less time than annual budgeting because you collect information as it is happening; your numbers will be more accurate; and you will be able to stay ahead of the 'change effect' on doing business and being in business.

"What will be the effect if you were to adapt a monthly planning and budgeting meetings for your business?"

Refer to *Profile the Numbers* below for more details

3 Use an Operating Budget Formula

The following will focus on the Business Operating Budget. Other budgets are important but the Operating Budget is used most often to plan and evaluate business activity. Topics will include:

- An Operating Budget Formula
- The Starting Point
- Building the Operating Budget
- Using the Budget Formula for a:
  o Service Business
  o Product Based Business
  o Business with Multiple Streams of Revenue
  o Not-for-profit Business

A **Business Operating Budget** is your **Business Operating Plan** presented in financial terms. **Its primary purpose is to show you how much revenue you will need to produce to sustain your Business Operating Plans.**

An Operating Budget Formula

$$MOR=KD\$/(1-(ADC\%+NPG\%))$$
Where

- MOR (Minimum Operating Revenue) = Revenue needed to sustain operations
- KD\$ (Known Disbursements) = Disbursements tied to being in business and to doing business. Payroll, Operating Expense, Capital Disbursements...
- ADC% (Average Direct Cost) as a percent of MOR for product(s) sold
- NPG% (Net Profit Goal) as a percent of MOR

Three Essential Business Tasks
A budget is your Operating Plan stated in financial terms

Scenario 1				Scenario 2			
Assumptions				**Assumptions**			
KD$	$ 75,000			KD$	$ 75,000		
ADC%	54.0%	0.0% if no product		ADC%	0.0%	0.0% if no product	
NPG%	8.0%			NPG%	8.0%		
MOR=KD$/(1-(ADC%+NPG%))				MOR=KD$/(1-(ADC%+NPG%))			
MOR	$ 197,368	100.0%		MOR	$ 81,522	100.0%	
DC	$ 106,579	54.0%		DC	$ -	0.0%	
GM	$ 90,789	46.0%		GM	$ 81,522	100.0%	
KD$	$ 75,000	38.0%		KD$	$ 75,000	92.0%	
NPG	$ 15,789	8.0%		NPG	$ 6,522	8.0%	

The advantage and disadvantage to using a formula

The speed at which you can:

- Determine the revenue you need to meet your goals;
- Recognize the effect of change;
- Create scenarios for potential change.

The disadvantage:

- Making decisions without the due diligence required to collect timely and accurate information.

The Starting Point

You can say you want to make a million dollars but if you do not have the capacity to reach the goal you can go broke trying.

Far too often budgeting begins with a revenue number – "How much do I want to make?"

How much you want to make is not the question you should be asking; the focus should be on how much you need to make and how much your capacity and business environment will allow you to make. The formula above will give you both but the MOR number is only as good as the numbers used in the formula.

Capacity: the numbers to the right of the equal sign.

Three Essential Business Tasks
A budget is your Operating Plan stated in financial terms

Sample Operating Budget Format	Annual $	% of MOR	Formula Assumptions
Revenue			
4100 Revenue 1	$ 172,059	65.0%	
4200 Revenue 2	$ 92,647	35.0%	
Total Revenue	$ 264,706	100.0%	
Direct Cost			
5100 Direct Cost 1	$ 99,794	37.7%	
5200 Direct Cost 2	$ 53,735	20.3%	
Total Direct Cost	$ 153,529	58.0%	ADC%
Gross Margin	$ 111,176	42.0%	
Operating Expense			
6100 Payroll & Related	$ 44,000	16.6%	
6500 Fixed Operating Exp	$ 22,000	8.3%	
7000 Variable Operating Exp	$ 13,000	4.9%	
Total Operating Exp	$ 79,000	29.8%	
Net Income from Operations	$ 32,176	12.2%	KD$
9100 Debt Retirement	$ 5,000	1.9%	
9200 Capital Expenditures	$ 6,000	2.3%	
Sub-total	$ 11,000	4.2%	
Total Operating Exp + Debt & Capital	$ 90,000	34.0%	
Net Profit Goal	$ 21,176	8%	NPG%

Building the Operating Budget

You can guess; you can use last year's numbers; or you can complete the due diligence necessary to build a timely and reliable Operating Budget by Identifying Financially Significant Numbers and Profiling the numbers before you use the formula.

Identify Financially Significant Numbers

Your Chart of Accounts is the resource you use to identify numbers you need to evaluate business activity. Refer to *Good Bookkeeping and Create a Functional Chart of Accounts* for details.

Profile the Numbers

Profiling here means to ask and answer questions that will give you the information you need to make informed decisions. Profiling takes time but once you have the critical details about each disbursement you will have a defined resource to help you make informed decisions and to simplify the future budgeting process.

The best approach is to create a Profile Worksheet and then use the worksheet on each disbursement you have identified. Here is a starter list of questions:

- What is the product or service name?
- What is the purpose of the product or service? Its use and benefit?
- Who will provide the product or service? Is there an alternative provider?
- Is there a warranty for the product or service?
- Is there a contract for the product or service? If yes, summarize the key components.
- How is cost calculated? i.e., product cost, shipping & handling, set-up...
- What is the amount? Annual and Monthly
- What is the payment schedule?
- What would be the affect if this product or service were eliminated? Use increased? Use decreased?
- When did you last do a review of this Product or Service?
- Is cost fixed or variable?
- General Ledger Account Number and Name

If you do your homework and adequately profile the budget numbers, you avoid random cuts, you will know the effect of cuts in your budget, and you will gain reasonable assurance of reliability.

The budget formula is only as good as the numbers used in the calculation. Details are Important but...

Revenue

Revenue is a calculated number based on the Operating Budget Formula. Once you have the MOR you can increase it to what the market will bear but you can't decrease it unless you decrease at least one of the capacity numbers (more on this under *Using the Budget Formula*).

Three Essential Business Tasks
A budget is your Operating Plan stated in financial terms

Direct Cost

This is the price you pay for product(s) you sell. In the Budget Formula it is expressed as a percent of the selling price or MOR. If you are selling one product the calculation is fairly simple (Cost / Selling Price). When you move into multiple products, discounting product... the calculation gets a bit tricky. We will get into the various scenarios and other issues with Direct Cost under *Using the Budget Formula*.

Revenue and Direct Cost are profiled on the same worksheet.

Salaries, Wages, & Related Expense

It is easy to miss expenses related to Salaries, Wages, and Related Expense if you don't know what to look for. Here is a worksheet to help capture all related expense:

Item	Amount	% of Total	Item	Hrs
Annual Wage	$ 40,000	80.98%	FTE	2080
Payroll Tax Expense			Overhead Hrs	
FICA	$ 3,060	6.20%	PTO	-120
FUTA	$ 64	0.13%	Holidays	-64
SUTA	$ 279	0.56%	Breaks	-59
SDI or Worker's Comp	$ 490	0.99%	Training	-16
Sub-total PR Tax Exp	$ 3,893	8%	Down Time	-429
Employee Benefit Exp			Total OH Hrs	-688
Medical	$ 5,500	11.14%	Available Hrs	1392
Other	$ -	0.00%		
Total Benefits	$ 5,500	11.14%		
Total Tax & Benefit Exp	$ 9,393	19.02%		
Total Wages & Exp	$ 49,393	100.00%		

You should profile each position within your business. The answer to the question, "What would be the affect if this (position) were ...?" can be a helpful evaluation tool.

Three Essential Business Tasks
A budget is your Operating Plan stated in financial terms

Operating Expense

Too much detail is to be avoided when creating a Functional Chart of Accounts. When you profile each ledger account though, details are very important. One ledger account could have a number of separate expense profiles. Remember to separate Fixed and Variable Expense. You do not need to include Non-cash transactions like Depreciation in the Operating Budget.

Balance Sheet Disbursements

You may be asking, "What are Balance Sheet Disbursements doing in an Operating Budget?" The answer is in the Operating Budget definition:

A Business Operating Budget is your Business Operating Plan presented in financial terms. Its primary purpose is to show you how much revenue you will need to produce to sustain your Business Operating Plans.

Debt Retirement and Cash layouts for Capital Purchases are two examples.

Yes, the Operating Budget could be considered a modified Cash Flow Budget also.

Net Profit Goal

Net Profit is the difference between Revenue and Disbursements. In the Operating Budget there are two Net Profit Numbers:

- Net Profit from operations – traditional Profit and Loss calculation;
- Net Profit Goal after all disbursements. This is the Formula NPG%.

How much money do you want to end up with after <u>all</u> is said and done?

Three Essential Business Tasks
A budget is your Operating Plan stated in financial terms

Saying you want a profit is not enough. You need a number and you need to know why the number you choose is with-in your capacity to generate. The number can be a fixed dollar amount (included in KD$) or a percent of revenue; or both.

What a Net Profit Goal should not include

Do not assume a wage for yourself or any partner in your business in your Net Profit Goal.

Why? Because you need to know what it cost to be in business; what it would cost to replace you or a partner should either decide to pursue another venture but want to keep the current business going.

Decide on a reasonable salary for what you do for the business. Then calculate the related payroll expense and post the number to your KD$'s.

What would you pay someone to do what you do? Use the Salaries, Wages, & Related Expense Worksheet presented earlier to calculate the number.

What a Net Profit Goal should include

In the Budget Formula the NPG% includes the sum of the following:

- PBD% - a Projected Bad Debt as a percent of MOR;
- WW% - Warranty Work as a percent of MOR;
- COM% - Commissions as a percent of MOR;
- NOP% - The Net Operating Profit as a percent of MOR.
- NPG% = PBD%+WW%+COM%+NOP%

PBD% - If you are going to allow customers to charge or delay payment for the products or services you sell, you are going to accrue bad debt – customers who do not pay. You need to estimate a percentage of MOR for the budget cycle and include the percent in your NPG%.

WW% - This number should include Warranty Work for Services and Returns for Products you sell. Estimate a % and include it in the NPG%.

COM% - If you have employees who are paid a bonus or commission for the work they perform, you need to estimate a percent of MOR and include the number in the NPG%.

NOP% - A Net Operating Profit should be a reasonable return on your investment of time, money, materials, and labor and/or an amount you need to expand business or maintain business during down cycles.

What is reasonable? Too high a return can create a negative response from customers; attract competition. Too low a return can prevent you from: expanding; rewarding you and employees for 'good work'. Too low can also prevent you from participating in community and humanitarian endeavors you have a passion to be a part of.

Why do you want a return of X$'s? What are you going to do with the return? You need to know.

Profits are what keep businesses alive; they are earned rewards for hard work on the part of the owner and the employees. They are the rewards investors seek. They are the resources a business can use to grow the business and support their community.

Define your Net Profit Goal

Take a clean sheet of paper and write at the top of the page, "My Net Profit Goal for (define the business cycle; usually a date range).

Next, profile the Net Profit Goal. State the goal as a percent of MOR or as a fixed dollar amount or both.

Define your rational for the goal. This statement should include how and why your business environment will or can support the goal; what you plan to do with the Net Income. This Net Profit Goal will probably change as you go through the budgeting process. But that is ok. At least you have a goal and a rational for the goal. Budgeting is about refining your goals and rational to fit reality.

For a very interesting perspective on 'profits – Net Income' read Michael Strong's "Be the Solution". Michael Strong is the founder and CEO of Whole Foods

Using the Formula

$$MOR = KD\$/(1-(ADC\% + NPG\%))$$

Where

- MOR (Minimum Operating Revenue) = Revenue needed to sustain operations
- KD\$ (Known Disbursements) = Disbursements tied to being in business and to doing business. Payroll, Operating Expense, Capital Disbursements...
- ADC% (Average Direct Cost) as a percent of MOR for product(s) sold
- NPG% (Net Profit Goal) as a percent of MOR

The following are examples of the formula at work in a variety of business settings.

- Service Based Business
- Product Based Business
- Business with multiple streams of revenue
- Not-for-Profit endeavor

Service Based Business

Billing Rate and Available or Billable Hours are keys to succeeding in a service business.

If your Billing rate is too high you could lose to competition; if your billing rate is too low you could lose your business. If you over estimate Billable Hours your Billing Rate will be too low; if you underestimate Billable Hours your Billing Rate will be too high. To determine the appropriate Billing Rate you will need to consider three questions:

Three Essential Business Tasks
A budget is your Operating Plan stated in financial terms

1. What are your Available Labor Hours (Billable Hours) for performing and billing service?
2. How much do you need to charge customers for your service?
3. How much can you charge?

Billable Hours

The following worksheet illustrates the calculation of Billable Hours.

Hours			
Item	Hrs	% of FTE	
FTE	2080	100.0%	1 FTE = 2080 hrs
Overhead Hrs			
PTO	-120	-5.8%	Vacation & Paid Sick Leave
Holidays	-64	-3.1%	
Breaks	-59	-2.8%	
Training	-16	-0.8%	
Down Time	-533	-25.6%	Travel, Admin Work, Warranty W
Total OH Hrs	-792	-38.1%	
Billable Hours	**1288**	**61.9%**	

It is very tempting to overstate the Available Billing Hours (ABH). It is much better to underestimate the number until you have enough experience to set a more accurate number. This number is used to calculate the Minimum Billing Rate for your services.

Minimum Billing Rate (MBR)

To determine a Minimum Billing Rate (MBR), divide MOR (Minimum Operating Revenue) by the Billable Hours for production employees.

Assumptions	1 FTE	2 FTE's	3 FTE's
Wages, Salaries, & Relate	$ 49,393	$ 98,786	$ 148,179
Operating Expense	$ 12,000	$ 14,000	$ 16,000
Total KD$	$ 61,393	$ 112,786	$ 164,179
NIG%	12.0%	12.0%	12.0%
ALH @ 64% of FTE	1331	2662	3994
MOR=KD$/(1-(ADC%+NIG%))			
MOR	$ 69,765	$ 128,166	$ 186,567
KD$	$ 61,393	$ 112,786	$ 164,179
NPG	$ 8,372	$ 15,380	$ 22,388
NPG%	12.0%	12.0%	12.0%
MBR (MOR / ALH)	$ 52.41	$ 48.14	$ 46.72

Three Essential Business Tasks
A budget is your Operating Plan stated in financial terms

You can increase the MBR to improve actual revenue but you cannot arbitrarily reduce the number and meet the budget requirements; the revenue required to sustain the business.

To reduce the MBR you will need to reduce capacity numbers or increase the Billable Hours. Note the change in the MBR when a second and third production employee is added.

If you are working solo do not assume you can work more than forty hours a week and bill more than twenty hours. You will, but don't budget with that assumption.

Keep the three questions in mind when determining your MBR.

1. What are your Billable Hours for performing and billing service?
2. How much do you need to charge customers for your service?
3. How much can you charge?

Product Based Business

You will need to deal with three questions when selling products.

1. How much will my business environment allow me to 'mark-up' cost? *Mark-up = Selling Price / Cost*
2. How many of product x do I need to sell? *MOR / Selling Price*
3. Is the quantity doable?

We will look at five scenarios:

1. Single Product purchased at cost with no selling price restrictions.
2. Selling one product at varying Mark-ups.
3. Selling Multiple Products purchased at the same discount.
4. Selling Multiple Products purchased at varying discounts.
5. The effect of discounting one product.

Three Essential Business Tasks
A budget is your Operating Plan stated in financial terms

#1 – Selling product purchased at cost with no price restriction

You have purchased a product at cost with no restrictions on the selling price and you want to know what you need to charge to meet your budget requirements.

1. Include the purchase cost in the KD$
2. Calculate the MOR
3. Determine the minimum Mark-up – MOR / Cost

Item	Amounts		Amounts	
KD$	$	41,000	$	41,000
Product Cost	$	25,000	$	50,000
Total KD$	$	**66,000**	$	**91,000**
ADC%		0.00%		0.00%
NPG%		12.50%		12.50%

MOR=KD$/(1-(ADC%+NPG%)) Note ADC%=0; DC is included in KD$					
MOR	$	75,429	100.0%	$	104,000	100.0%
DC	$	25,000	33.1%	$	50,000	48.1%
Gross Margin	$	50,429	66.9%	$	54,000	51.9%
KD$ less Product Cost	$	41,000	54.4%	$	41,000	39.4%
NPG	$	9,429	12.5%	$	13,000	12.5%
Minimum Mark-up		301.7% MOR / DC			208.0% MOR / DC

Note what happens to the Mark-up when you purchase more product. Sometimes to get the selling price down you will need to increase your initial purchase.

When investigating a business opportunity, this worksheet can help you determine if the business is doable. When competition is high, price becomes an important factor also. Therefore, know what you are going to have to invest is a critical part of you decision making process.

Three Essential Business Tasks
A budget is your Operating Plan stated in financial terms

#2 - Selling one product at varying Mark-ups

	Product A	Product A	Product A
ADC Change w/Selling Price Change			
Selling $	$ 38.00	$ 36.00	$ 30.00
Cost	$ 19.000	$ 19.000	$ 19.000
ADC%	50.0%	52.8%	63.3%
Mark-up	200.0%	189.5%	157.9%
Operating Budget Formula Assumptions			
KD$	$ 61,393	$ 61,393	$ 61,393
ADC%	50%	53%	63%
NIG%	12%	12%	12%
	Product A	Product A	Product A
MOR by Prod	$ 161,561	$ 174,302	$ 248,891
Prod Cost	$ 80,780	$ 91,993	$ 157,631
Gross Margin	$ 80,780	$ 82,309	$ 91,260
KD$	$ 61,393	$ 61,393	$ 61,393
NPG	$ 19,387	$ 20,916	$ 29,867
NPG%	12.0%	12.0%	12.0%
Quantity	4,252	4,842	8,296

Note the change in the ADC%, the Mark-up, and the quantity. The key question, "Is the quantity doable?

Also, remember you can't arbitrarily change the MOR number because it is controlled by the numbers to the right of the equal sign. The NPG% is the simplest to change but remember what a Net Profit is for. So think seriously about why you are in business before you make changes.

There are a whole lot of internet business opportunities out there. Before you jump into one of the opportunities, use the Operating Budget Formula to test a variety of scenarios to see what being in business and doing business really means.

#3 - Selling multiple products purchased at the same discount

This scenario requires a bit more calculating. You will need a Revenue Mix % to calculate Product MOR then Quantity (**Revenue Mix** = the percent of revenue each product is <u>expected</u> to contribute.)

Three Essential Business Tasks
A budget is your Operating Plan stated in financial terms

ADC% with Multiple Products at the same Discount

	Product A	Product B	Product C	
Selling $	$ 38.00	$ 26.00	$ 13.00	
Discount	50%	50%	50%	
Cost	$ 19.00	$ 13.00	$ 6.50	ADC%
DC% --> ADC%	50%	50%	50%	50%
Mark-up	200%	200%	200%	
Revenue Mix %	20%	40%	40%	

Operating Budget Formula Assumptions

KD$	$ 61,393			
ADC%	50%	MOR=	$ 161,561	
NPG%	12%			

	Product A	Product B	Product C	Total
MOR by Prod (MOR * RM%)	$ 31,646	$ 64,957	$ 64,957	$ 161,561
Prod Cost	$ 15,823	$ 32,479	$ 32,479	$ 80,780
Gross Margin	$ 15,823	$ 32,479	$ 32,479	$ 80,780
KD$				$ 61,393
NPG%			12.0%	$ 19,387
Quantity	833	2,498	4,997	

If you have a large inventory you may want to list product in categories to complete the calculations.

Remember the key question, "is the quantity doable?".

Three Essential Business Tasks
A budget is your Operating Plan stated in financial terms

#4 - Product with multiple purchase discounts

This scenario creates a bit more work. Note the ADC% Calculation.

Products with multiple purchase discounts			
	Product A	Product B	Product C
Selling $	$ 38.00	$ 26.00	$ 13.00	
Discount	50%	45%	35%	
Cost	$ 19.00	$ 14.30	$ 8.45	ADC%
DC% --> ADC%	50%	55%	65%	58.0%
Revenue Mix	20%	40%	40%	

ADC% = The sum of Product DC% * Product Revenue Mix%
ADC%=((.50*.20)+(.55*.40)+(.65*.40))

Operating Budget Formula Assumptions				
KD$	$ 61,393			
ADC%	58%	MOR=	$ 204,925	
NPG%	12%			
	Product A	Product B	Product C	Total
MOR by Prod (MOR*RM%)	$ 40,140	$ 82,393	$ 82,393	$ 204,925
Prod Cost	$ 20,070	$ 45,316	$ 53,555	$ 118,941
Gross Margin	$ 20,070	$ 37,077	$ 28,837	$ 85,984
KD$				$ 61,393
NPG			12.0%	$ 24,591
Quantity	1,056	3,169	6,338	

It is important to remember to consider these three questions in either scenario.

1. How much will my business environment allow me to 'mark-up' cost? *Mark-up = Selling Price / Cost*
2. How many of product x do I need to sell? *MOR / Selling Price*
3. Is the quantity doable?

#5 – The effect of discounting a product

Offering product discounts and 'loss leaders' creates a bit more work yet. This is one reason you should refine your budget for the month you are planning a sale.

We will use Product C from the previous example as the 'loss leader' in this example. The purpose of a loss leader is to gain customer traffic and potentially sell more of other products.

In this example, for every Product A you sell you are offering a 50% discount on Product C. Your goal is to improve customer traffic and double Product A Sales. The worksheet and formula will help you determine if the plan is workable.

Note the change in Product A Cost

- $19.00 Product A Cost
- $ 8.95 Product C Cost
- $- 6.50 Product C Sell Price @ 50%
- $21.45 Product A Adjusted Cost

Product A carries the cost of the 'sale'. You are still selling product C at the normal price.

The Budget Formula shows you the Minimum Operating Revenue and product quantities required to meet budget goals. The key question is still, "Is the quantity doable?"

Products with multiple purchase discounts	Product A	Product B	Product C	
Selling $	$ 38.00	$ 26.00	$ 13.00	
Discount	50%	45%	35%	
Cost	$ 21.45	$ 14.30	$ 8.45	ADC%
DC% --> ADC%	56%	55%	65%	57.6%
Revenue Mix	40%	40%	20%	

ADC% = The sum of Product DC% * Product Revenue Mix%
ADC%=((.56*.40)+(.55*.40)+(.65*.20))

Operating Budget Formula Assumptions

KD$	$ 61,393			
ADC%	57.6%	MOR=	$ 201,811	
NPG%	12%			
	Product A	Product B	Product C	Total
MOR by Prod	$ 80,724	$ 80,724	$ 40,362	$ 201,811
Prod Cost	$ 45,567	$ 44,398	$ 26,235	$ 116,201
Gross Margin	$ 35,158	$ 36,326	$ 14,127	$ 85,610
KD$				$ 61,393
NPG			12.0%	$ 24,217
Quantity	2,124	3,105	3,105	

As you gain experience you will be adjusting the Sales Mix % to help reflect more precise budget projections.

Business with Multiple Streams of Revenue

This is where fun and patience really begins. You are going to need several worksheets but once they are formulated the process of calculating MOR is fairly simple.

A business with multiple streams of revenue is usually divided into departments. When calculating MOR, you will first consider each department as a separate business sharing overhead expenses; then you consolidate the budgets to create the Business Operating Budget.

Three Essential Business Tasks
A budget is your Operating Plan stated in financial terms

For this example we will assume an Equipment Sales, Installation, and Service business with four departments:

- Administrative,
- Equipment Sales & Installation,
- Service,
- Parts/Warehouse.

Five Step Process

Calculating MOR for a business with multiple streams of income is a six step process:

- Step 1 – List and Profile the KD$;
- Step 2 – Distribute Direct KD$ to departments;
- Step 3 – Allocate Overhead.
- Step 4 – Combine the Direct KD$ and the Overhead amounts
- Step 5 – Apply the Operating Budget Formula to each department;

Some of the information on the following worksheet in hidden in order to keep the worksheet on one page.

Three Essential Business Tasks
A budget is your Operating Plan stated in financial terms

Step 1 - List & Profile KD$

Wages, Salaries, & Related	Total				
Wages & Salaries	$ 275,000				
Payroll Taxes	$ 23,030				
Worker's Comp	$ 30,870				
Employee Benefits	$ 42,000				
Total Payroll	**$ 370,900**				
Fixed Operating Expense					
Staff Development	$ 12,000				
Office & Whse Lease	$ 30,000				
Building Maintenance Cont	$ 5,600		Create a Profile Worksheet		
Business & Vehicle Insurance	$ 20,000		for each line item on the		
Office Equipment Lease	$ 7,000		budget worksheet. Some line		
Telephone Land Lines & Cell Phone	$ 5,060		itrems may have multiple		
Internet Service Provider	$ 900		profiles.		
Total Fixed Operating Exp	**$ 80,560**				
Variable Operating Exp			This list does not necessarily		
Utilities	$ 14,400		have to be the final Chart of		
Office Supplies	$ 3,600		Accounts. You can roll up line		
Postage, UPS, Fed Ex Expense	$ 4,600		items summarizing related		
Shipping Supplies	$ 3,500		transactions.		
Telephone Excess Use Fees	$ 1,200				
Office Equip Maintenance	$ 1,350				
Vehicle Fuel Exp	$ 27,000				
Vehicle Maintenance Exp	$ 6,000				
Employee Expense Reimbursemen	$ 8,300				
Total Variable Operating Exp	**$ 69,950**				
Total Operating Expense	**$ 150,510**				
Balance Sheet Disbursements					
Auto Loans	$ 22,000				
Bank Credit Line	$ 10,000				
Total Debt Retirement	**$ 32,000**				
Total All Disbursements	**$ 553,410**				

Three Essential Business Tasks

A budget is your Operating Plan stated in financial terms

Step 2 – Distribute Direct KD$ to departments;

This distribution is based on expenses that can be directly tied to each department. Any residual is posted to the Administrative Department – Business Overhead.

Wages, Salaries, & Related	Total	Sales & Installation	Service	Parts & Whse	Total to Production	Admin Overhead
Wages & Salaries	$ 275,000	$ 45,000	$ 80,000	$ 35,000	$ 160,000	$ 115,000
Payroll Taxes	$ 23,030	$ 3,775	$ 6,452	$ 3,010	$ 13,236	$ 9,794
Worker's Comp	$ 30,870	$ 9,675	$ 17,200	$ 2,730	$ 29,605	$ 1,265
Employee Benefits	$ 42,000	$ 6,000	$ 12,000	$ 6,000	$ 24,000	$ 18,000
Total Payroll	**$ 370,900**	**$ 64,450**	**$ 115,652**	**$ 46,740**	**$ 226,841**	**$ 144,059**
Fixed Operating Expense						
Staff Development	$ 12,000	$ 1,666	$ 1,666	$ 1,666	$ 4,998	$ 7,002
Office & Whse Lease	$ 30,000	$ 1,000	$ 1,000	$ 16,000	$ 18,000	$ 12,000
Building Maintenance Cont	$ 5,600	$ 250	$ 250	$ 1,500	$ 2,000	$ 3,600
Business & Vehicle Insuran	$ 20,000	$ 3,000	$ 4,500	$ 3,000	$ 10,500	$ 9,500
Total Fixed Operating Exp	**$ 80,560**	**$ 6,716**	**$ 9,016**	**$ 22,966**	**$ 38,698**	**$ 41,862**
Variable Operating Exp						
Utilities	$ 14,400	$ -	$ -	$ 8,400	$ 8,400	$ 6,000
Office Supplies	$ 3,600	$ -	$ -	$ -	$ -	$ 3,600
Postage, UPS, Fed Ex Expens	$ 4,600	$ -	$ -	$ 3,000	$ 3,000	$ 1,600
Vehicle Maintenance Exp	$ 6,000	$ 1,250	$ 2,500	$ 1,250	$ 5,000	$ 1,000
Employee Expense Reimbur	$ 8,300	$ 600	$ 1,200	$ 600	$ 2,400	$ 5,900
Total Variable Operating Exp	**$ 69,950**	**$ 8,050**	**$ 12,900**	**$ 20,950**	**$ 41,900**	**$ 28,050**
Total Operating Expense	**$ 150,510**	**$ 14,766**	**$ 21,916**	**$ 43,916**	**$ 80,598**	**$ 69,912**
Balance Sheet Disbursements						
Auto Loans	$ 22,000	$ 4,620	$ 9,240	$ 4,620	$ 18,480	$ 3,520
Bank Credit Line	$ 10,000	$ -	$ -	$ -	$ -	$ 10,000
Total Debt Retirement	**$ 32,000**	**$ 4,620**	**$ 9,240**	**$ 4,620**	**$ 18,480**	**$ 13,520**
Total All Disbursements	**$ 553,410**	**$ 83,836**	**$ 146,808**	**$ 95,276**	**$ 325,919**	**$ 227,491**

Step 3 – Allocate Overhead.

Overhead includes all expenses posted to the Administrative Department. There are two approaches to accomplishing this task. Each method uses the Production Departments FTE Hours. When allocating Overhead you want to use a number that remains constant during the budget cycle. FTE Hours is usually the best number.

Overhead Allocation Rate (OAR) method. This is a summary approach. Calculate the OAR then multiply Department FTE Hours * OAR.

	Sales & Install	Service	Parts & Whse	Total	
Production FTE Hours	2080	4160	2080	8320	
OAR by Expense Categories		Total OH			
Payroll		$ 144,059		$	17.31
Fixed Expene		$ 41,862		$	4.76
Variable Expense		$ 28,050		$	2.65
Balance Sheet Transactions		$ 13,520		$	1.63
OAR=OH / Total Production Hours ($227491/8320)		$ 227,491	OAR -->	$	27.34

	Total	Sales & Install.	Service	Whse	Admin OH
FTE Labor Hours For Production		2080	4160	2080	8320
Overhead Allocation Rate		$ 27.34	$ 27.34	$ 27.34	$ 27.34
Overhead Allocation		$ 56,873	$ 113,745	$ 56,873	$ (227,491)

Using this method you would insert an Overhead Line below the major sub totals or before the NPG.

Production FTE Hours Percent method. This is a detailed approach.

- Determine the FTE Hour Percent for each Production Department - divide the Department's FTE Hours by the Total Production FTE number.
- Apply the Percent to each line item.

Three Essential Business Tasks
A budget is your Operating Plan stated in financial terms

Direct Operating Expense		25%	50%	25%	
By percent of FTE		Sales & Ins Service		Parts & Whse	
Production FTE Hours		2080	4160	2080	8320
Production FTE Hours %		25%	50%	25%	
Department's FTE Hours / Total Production FTE Hours = %					

Line #	Wages, Salaries, & Related	Admin Overhead	Sales & Installatin	Service	Parts & Whse	Check Sum
3	Wages & Salaries	$ 115,000	$ 28,750	$ 57,500	$ 28,750	$ 115,000
4	Payroll Taxes	$ 9,794	$ 2,448	$ 4,897	$ 2,448	$ 9,794
5	Worker's Comp	$ 1,265	$ 316	$ 633	$ 316	$ 1,265
6	Employee Benefits	$ 18,000	$ 4,500	$ 9,000	$ 4,500	$ 18,000
7	**Total Payroll**	**$ 144,059**	**$ 36,015**	**$ 72,029**	**$ 36,015**	**$ 144,059**
8	**Fixed Operating Expense**					
9	Staff Development	$ 7,002	$ 1,751	$ 3,501	$ 1,751	$ 7,002
10	Office & Whse Lease	$ 12,000	$ 3,000	$ 6,000	$ 3,000	$ 12,000
12	Building Maintenance Cont	$ 3,600	$ 900	$ 1,800	$ 900	$ 3,600
13	Business & Vehicle Insurance	$ 9,500	$ 2,375	$ 4,750	$ 2,375	$ 9,500
15	Office Equipment Lease	$ 7,000	$ 1,750	$ 3,500	$ 1,750	$ 7,000
16	Telephone Land Lines & Cell Phor	$ 1,860	$ 465	$ 930	$ 465	$ 1,860
20	Internet Service Provider	$ 900	$ 225	$ 450	$ 225	$ 900
21	**Total Fixed Operating Exp**	**$ 41,862**	**$ 10,466**	**$ 20,931**	**$ 10,466**	**$ 41,862**
22	**Variable Operating Exp**					
23	Utilities	$ 6,000	$ 1,500	$ 3,000	$ 1,500	$ 6,000
24	Office Supplies	$ 3,600	$ 900	$ 1,800	$ 900	$ 3,600
25	Postage, UPS, Fed Ex Expense	$ 1,600	$ 400	$ 800	$ 400	$ 1,600
26	Shipping Supplies	$ 500	$ 125	$ 250	$ 125	$ 500
27	Telephone Excess Use Fees	$ 600	$ 150	$ 300	$ 150	$ 600
28	Office Equip Maintenance	$ 1,350	$ 338	$ 675	$ 338	$ 1,350
29	Vehicle Fuel Exp	$ 7,500	$ 1,875	$ 3,750	$ 1,875	$ 7,500
30	Vehicle Maintenance Exp	$ 1,000	$ 250	$ 500	$ 250	$ 1,000
31	Employee Expense Reimbursemer	$ 5,900	$ 1,475	$ 2,950	$ 1,475	$ 5,900
33	**Total Variable Operating Exp**	**$ 28,050**	**$ 5,513**	**$ 11,025**	**$ 5,513**	**$ 28,050**
34	**Total Operating Expense**	**$ 69,912**	**$ 15,978**	**$ 31,956**	**$ 15,978**	**$ 69,912**
35	**Balance Sheet Disbursements**					
37	Auto Loans	$ 3,520	$ 880	$ 1,760	$ 880	$ 3,520
38	Bank Credit Line	$ 10,000	$ 2,500	$ 5,000	$ 2,500	$ 10,000
39	**Total Debt Retirement**	**$ 13,520**	**$ 3,380**	**$ 6,760**	**$ 3,380**	**$ 13,520**
40	**Total All Disbursements**	**$ 227,491**	**$ 55,373**	**$ 110,745**	**$ 55,373**	**$ 227,491**

Three Essential Business Tasks
A budget is your Operating Plan stated in financial terms

Step 4 – Combine the Direct KD$ and the Overhead amounts

Direct Expense					
Payroll	$ 370,901	$ 64,450	$ 115,652	$ 46,740	$ 144,059
Fixed OPE	$ 80,560	$ 6,716	$ 9,016	$ 22,966	$ 41,862
Variable OPE	$ 69,950	$ 8,050	$ 12,900	$ 20,950	$ 28,050
Balance Sheet	$ 32,000	$ 4,620	$ 9,240	$ 4,620	$ 13,520
Total	$ 553,411	$ 83,836	$ 146,808	$ 95,276	$ 227,491
FTE Hours	8,320	2,080	4,160	2,080	
OAR		$ 27.34	$ 27.34	$ 27.34	
Overhead Allocation		$ 56,867	$ 113,734	$ 56,867	$ (227,491)
Total KD$	$ 553,411	$ 140,703	$ 260,542	$ 152,165	$ -

Step 5 – Apply the Operating Budget Formula to each department

	Total	Sales & Install	Service	Parts & Whse	Admin OH
Total KD$ -->	$ 553,410	$ 140,703	$ 260,542	$ 152,165	$ -
ADC%		67.0%	0.0%	52.0%	
NPG%		6.0%	8.0%	15.0%	
MOR=KD$/(1-(ADC%+NPG%))					
MOR =	$ 1,265,426	$ 521,122	$ 283,198	$ 461,106	

	Total	Sales & Install.	Service	Whse	Admin OH
MOR	$ 1,265,406	$ 521,141	$ 283,210	$ 461,055	
Direct Cost	$ 588,913	$ 349,165	$ -	$ 239,749	
Gross Margin	$ 676,493	$ 171,977	$ 283,210	$ 221,306	
Payroll Expense	$ 370,900	$ 64,450	$ 115,652	$ 46,740	$ 144,059
Fixed	$ 80,560	$ 6,716	$ 9,016	$ 22,966	$ 41,862
Variable	$ 69,950	$ 8,050	$ 12,900	$ 20,950	$ 28,050
Overhead Allocatin	$ -	$ 53,493	$ 106,985	$ 53,493	$ (213,971)
Total OPE	$ 521,410	$ 132,708	$ 244,553	$ 144,148	$ -
Net Operating P	$ 155,084	$ 39,268	$ 38,657	$ 77,158	
NOP %	12.3%	7.5%	13.6%	16.7%	
Balance Sheet Dist	$ 18,480	$ 4,620	$ 9,240	$ 4,620	$ 13,520
Overhead Allocatio	$ -	$ 3,380	$ 6,760	$ 3,380	$ (13,520)
NPG	$ 136,604	$ 31,268	$ 22,657	$ 69,158	$ -
NPG%	10.8%	6.0%	8.0%	15.0%	

Three Essential Business Tasks

A budget is your Operating Plan stated in financial terms

Two additional tasks

Once you have the Operating Budget there are two additional tasks:

1. Calculate a Minimum Billing Rate for Service (MBR)
2. Calculate a Minimum Labor Rate and the ADC% for bidding installation work.

Service Department Billing Rate

Divide the Service Department MOR by the Service Department Available Labor Hours (ALH). We are assuming ALH @ 65% of FTE.

- 4160 FTE Hours * 65% - 2704
- $283210 Service MOR / 2704 ALH = $104.75 MBR

Remember, you cannot 'arbitrarily' lower the rate but you can increase the rate. You may be able to lower the rate by increasing the ALH. Be careful though. Do a 'what if' calculation for adding a new employee.

Equipment Installation Labor Rate & ADC%

Two important issues when you are selling and installing equipment:

1. Installation Labor Rate
2. ADC% Calculation

Installation Labor Rate

This is the hourly rate you will use in bidding a project so that each project bears a proportionate share of the Departments' Overhead Expense (Direct Expense + Overhead Allocation).

Divide the Total Department Expense (Direct and Overhead Allocation) by the ALH (Available Labor Hours) of your Installation Staff.

Dept Direct Expense + OH Allocation	$ 140,709.0
ALH @ 65% of FTE	1352
Install Labor Rate	$ 104.07

ADC% Calculation

The ADC% you use in the Budget Formula is based on a 'standard' Equipment Install.

Equipment Cost	$	5,000	
Support Materials	$	1,000	
Total	$	**6,000**	66.8% ADC%
Estimated Labor Hours		20	
Labor Rate	$	104	
Labor Cost	$	**2,080**	
Total Install Cost	$	**8,080**	
NPG%		10%	
Minimum Bid Price (MBP)	$	8,978	

Budgeting is an educated guess. Not all installations will have the same ADC% but you need a number to start with. Time and experience will provide better numbers.

ALH (Available Labor Hours) from your installation employees will limit the number of units you can install and will have a +/- effect on Revenue. In the above example ALH = 1352 will limit you to 67 Units (1352/20) and the MOR = $605K (67*$8956). In this case the Revenue is greater than the MOR calculation. Use the MOR calculation for your budget. Always stay conservative.

Not-for-Profit Business

Many people think that a Not-for-Profit venture does not work on the same platform as a for-profit venture. Not true. The smart Not-for-Profit organizations want and need a 'Net Profit Goal' if they are going to be able to maintain operations in tough times. They just call the number by a different name – a Residual.

The budget formula

The budget formula is a little different.

$$MOR=KD\$/KD\%$$
Where

MOR=Minimum Operating Revenue

KD$ = Known Disbursements

KD$% = a set percent for KD$ or Overhead

KD$% is a set level usually 25% or below of MOR. Not-for-Profits are evaluated on this percentage. They are considered to be an efficient and effective organization if they keep their Overhead at or below the 25% mark.

Determining KD$'s

There are two ways to deal with KD$'s for a Not-for-Profit business:

1. Use Total KD$'s;
2. Project the % of employee labor that will be spent on Mission Based Programs & Projects and deduct the expense from KD$'s. Then use the adjusted KD$ as your base for calculating MOR. Cost for Mission Based Projects and Programs are not considered Overhead.

KD$	$	500,000	$	500,000
Labor Adj	$	(45,500)	$	–
Adj KD$	$	454,500	$	500,000
KD$%		20%		20%
MOR=	$	2,272,500	$	2,500,000

Three Essential Business Tasks
A budget is your Operating Plan stated in financial terms

The MOR is your fundraising goal; monies to use to cover Overheads and for Mission Based Programs and Projects. You may need more revenue to cover all of your Mission Based Projects and Programs but the formula MOR is the minimum to maintain budget goals; KD$% in particular.

Fundraising

Fundraising is usually considered a part of Overhead. Therefore, any cost not included in the KD$ used in the formula directly related to Fundraising should be divided by the KD$% number to determine how much revenue the Fundraising Project will need to generate to cover that cost and keep the KD$% Goal.

So you hire a Professional Fundraiser who contracts with you for $50,000. You can inform them that they will need to raise a minimum of $200K ($50,000/.25 = $200,000) to cover their cost. Any additional Fundraising Project Cost will need to meet the same criteria.

Projects & Programs

Projects and Programs are how a Not-for-Project fulfills its mission. You do not need project budgets in place to determine the MOR needed to maintain budget goals (KD%). If additional funds are needed as you progress, that becomes a Fundraising Budget issue (see *Fundraising* above).

To determine the Revenue needed to support a project or program you will need three numbers:

1. Estimated Staff Time
2. An Overhead Allocation Number (OAN)
3. Estimated Direct Cost

Three Essential Business Tasks
A budget is your Operating Plan stated in financial terms

Estimating Staff Time

How many hours will paid staff spend working on the project – planning, implementing, and evaluating. Like a for-profit business, you are limited to Available Labor Hours (ALH).

	Hours		
Item	Hrs	% of FTE	
FTE	2080	100.0%	1 FTE = 2080 hrs
Overhead Hrs			
PTO	-120	-5.8%	Vacation & Paid Sick Leave
Holidays	-64	-3.1%	
Breaks	-59	-2.8%	
Training	-16	-0.8%	
Down Time	-729	-35.0%	Travel, Admin Work, Fundraising
Total OH Hrs	-988	-47.5%	
Available Hrs	1092	52.5%	

An Overhead Allocation Number

Divide the KD$ by ALH to get this number.

Assumptions	
KD$	$ 500,000
ALH (5 FTE's @ 52.5%)	5460
OAN	$ 92

Estimated Direct Cost

These are disbursements directly related to the specific project. i.e., Promotion, Printing, Mailing, Facility, Catering…. Create a Profile worksheet for estimating these costs. Then file the worksheets for future use. You will save a great deal of time on future projects.

Project Budget Calculation

Assumptions		
KD$	$	500,000
ALH (5 FTE's @ 65%)		6760
OAN	$	92
Direct Project Cost	$	340,000
Estimated Staff Labor Hrs		400
Estimated OH Allocation (Hours *	$	36,800
Total Project Cost	**$**	**376,800**

The Total Project Cost is part of the MOR; your fundraising goal – a reason for the goal. Mission based Program and Project Direct Cost are not considered Overhead. They use MOR.

Budgeting Summary

Budgeting is not easy but it can be simplified with a little work up front. Once you have worksheets set, and your 'capacity' numbers – KD$, ADC% and NPG% - defined and profiled, adjusting for change is a fairly simple process using an Operating Budget Formula.

Having reliable numbers is the key. Identify and profile your capacity numbers and you will have a meaningful budget for evaluating operations and projecting the effect of change on your business venture.

Budgeting is not a once a year task. Shorten the budget cycles and you will improve your ability to quickly adjust to changes in your business environment.

Good Bookkeeping and Timely Planning are the foundation for Reliable Budgeting.

Conclusion

The only secret to success in business is working smart; doing the right things at the appropriate time correctly. Good Bookkeeping, Timely Planning, and Reliable Budgeting are three of the right things.

I have presented no guarantees to success but I can assure you that if you will get a handle on these three tasks you will have reached the road that leads to succeeding in your business venture.

Three Essential Business Tasks
A budget is your Operating Plan stated in financial terms

www.ingramcontent.com/pod-product-compliance
Lightning Source LLC
Chambersburg PA
CBHW071118210326
41519CB00020B/6342